Robert Fulghum was bo[...]
several academic degrees[...]
important in comparison to the education I've gotten on
my own.'

Throughout college and graduate school, Fulghum
worked as a singing cowboy in guest ranches in Texas,
Colorado and Montana, and rode in local rodeos. He has
also found employment as an IBM salesperson, a bar-
tender, and a folk music teacher. He plays guitar, bass and
mando'cello. He is an accomplished painter and has had
several successful showings of his work. For the past
twenty years he has taught drawing and painting at the
Lakeside School in Seattle.

For twenty-five years, he was also an ordained minister at
Seattle's Edmonds Unitarian Church, where he is now
minister emeritus. Fulghum has travelled twice around the
world, living for a time in Thailand, Greece, Japan (in a
Zen Buddhist monastery) and France. He now lives on a
houseboat in Seattle and spends his leisure time sailing.

By the same author

All I Really Need to Know I Learned in Kindergarten

ROBERT FULGHUM

It Was On Fire When I Lay Down On It

Grafton
An Imprint of HarperCollinsPublishers

GraftonBooks
A Division of HarperCollins*Publishers*
77–85 Fulham Palace Road,
Hammersmith, London W6 8JB

Published by GraftonBooks 1991

First published in USA by
Villard Books 1989

Two of the essays in this book were also previously
published in the USA in *Redbook,* and one in *Washington*

A CIP catalogue record for this book
is available from the British Library

ISBN 0-586-20952-2

Printed in Great Britain by
HarperCollinsManufacturing, Glasgow

Set in Bembo

I believe that imagination is stronger than knowledge—
That myth is more potent than history.
I believe that dreams are more powerful than facts—
That hope always triumphs over experience—
That laughter is the only cure for grief.
And I believe that love is stronger than death.

Show-and-Tell was the very best part of school for me, both as a student and as a teacher. Not recess or lunch, but that special time set aside each week for students to bring something important of their own to class to share and talk about.

As a kid, I put more into getting ready for my turn to present than I put into the rest of my homework. Show-and-Tell was *real* in a way that much of what I learned in school was not. It was education that came out of my life experience. And there weren't a lot of rules about Show-and-Tell—you could do your thing without getting red-penciled or dismissed to your seat.

As a teacher, I was always surprised by what I learned from these amateur hours. A kid I was sure I knew well would reach down into the paper bag he carried and fish out some odd-shaped treasure and attach meaning to it beyond my most extravagant expectation. It was me, the teacher, who was being taught at such moments.

Again and again I learned that what I thought was only true for me . . . only valued by me . . . only cared about by me . . . was common property.

Show-and-Tell was a bit disorderly and unpredictable. What the presentations lacked in conventional structure was compensated for by passion for the subject at hand.

The principles guiding this book are not far from the spirit of Show-and-Tell. It is my stuff from home—that place in my mind and heart where I most truly live. This volume picks up where I left off in *All I Really Need to Know I Learned in Kindergarten*, when I promised to tell about the time it was on fire when I lay down on it.

The form of this book is a reflection of the life from which it is drawn; here is not a collection of well-crafted essays, but the ongoing minutes from a one-man committee meeting, gussied up a bit for bringing to class. An amateur's job. I would read these pages to you if I could, but since that's not possible, I have a suggestion that verges on a request. You know how it is when you get a letter in the mail from a friend far away and you tear it open and start reading it and somebody else in the room says "Read it out loud" and you do and you talk about it as you go along, adding your own observations and explanations? Read it like that. Show and tell.

—Robert Fulghum

It Was on Fire
When I Lay
Down on It

A TABLOID NEWSPAPER CARRIED THE STORY, stating simply that a small-town emergency squad was summoned to a house where smoke was pouring from an upstairs window. The crew broke in and found a man in a smoldering bed. After the man was rescued and the mattress doused, the obvious question was asked: "How did this happen?"

"I don't know. It was on fire when I lay down on it."

The story stuck like a burr to my mental socks. And reminded me of a phrase copied into my journal from the dedication of some book: *"Quid rides? Mutato nomine, de te fabula narratur."* Latin. From the writings of Horace. Translated: "Why do you laugh? Change the name, and the story is told of you."

It was on fire when I lay down on it.

A lot of us could settle for that on our tombstones. A life-story in a sentence. Out of the frying pan and into the hot water. I was looking for trouble and got into it as soon as I found it. The devil made me do it the first time, and after that I did it on my own.

Or to point at this truth at a less intense level, I report a conversation with a colleague who was complaining that he had the same damn stuff in his lunch sack day after day.

"So who makes your lunch?" I asked.

"I do," says he.

We've got some fine old company in this deal.

Saint Paul bemoaned the fact that "I cannot understand my own behavior. I fail to carry out the things I want to do, and I find myself doing the very things I hate."

And the Greek dramatist Euripides puts these words in Medea's mouth just before she murders her own children: "I know what evil I am about to do. My irrational self is stronger than my resolution."

Psychiatrists make a lot of money off this dilemma, and theologians make a lot of noise. But not only is it unresolved, it is unresolvable. One lives with the dilemma, and in the living takes comfort in the company of those who habitually lie down on burning beds of one kind or another. It would be better if we could simply lay claim to the beds we choose as our own and get on with it.

And one more thing.

About the man in the burning bed in the story. As with most of what we see other people do, we don't know *why* they do it, either. If our own actions are mysteries, how much so others'? Why did he lie down on the burning bed? Was he drunk? Ill? Suicidal? Blind? Cold? Dumb? Did he just have a weird sense of humor? Or what? I don't know. It's hard to judge without a lot more information. Oh sure, we go ahead and judge anyhow. But maybe if judgment were suspended a bit more often, we would like us more.

God, it is written, warned his first children, Adam and Eve. He made it clear. Don't eat that piece of fruit—it will lead to trouble. You know the rest of the story. . . .

And part of that story is here in this book.

I HAVE MARRIED MORE THAN A THOUSAND TIMES. Officiated as the minister at a whole lot of weddings and usually managed to get so involved in each occasion that it felt like I was the one getting married. Still, I always look forward to marrying again, because most weddings are such comedies.

Not that they are intended as such. But since weddings are high state occasions involving amateurs under pressure, everything NEVER goes right. Weddings seem to be magnets for mishap and for whatever craziness lurks in family closets. In more ways than one, weddings bring out the ding-dong in everybody involved.

I will tell you the quintessential wedding tale. One of disaster. Surprisingly, it has a happy ending, though you may be in doubt, as I was, as the story unfolds.

The central figure in this drama was the mother of

the bride (MOTB). Not the bride and groom or minister. Mother. Usually a polite, reasonable, intelligent, and sane human being, Mother was mentally unhinged by the announcement of her daughter's betrothal. I don't mean she was unhappy, as is often the case. To the contrary. She was overcome with joy. And just about succeeded in overcoming everybody else with her joy before the dust settled.

Nobody knew it, but this lady had been waiting with a script for a production that would have met with Cecil B. DeMille's approval. A royal wedding fit for a princess bride. And since it was her money, it was hard to say no. The father of the bride began to pray for an elopement. His prayers were not to be answered.

She had seven months to work, and no detail was left to chance or human error. Everything that could be engraved was engraved. There were teas and showers and dinners. The bride and groom I met with only three times. The MOTB called me weekly, and was in my office as often as the cleaning lady. (*The caterer called me to ask if this was really a wedding, or an invasion he was involved in. "Invasion," I told him.*)

An eighteen-piece brass and wind ensemble was engaged. (*The church organ simply would not do—too "churchy."*) The bride's desires for home furnishings were registered in stores as far east as New York and as far south as Atlanta. Not only were the bridesmaids' outfits made to order, but the tuxedos for the groom and his men were bought—not rented, mind you. Bought. If all that wasn't enough, the engagement ring was returned to the jeweler for a larger stone, quietly subsidized by the MOTB. When I say the lady came unhinged, I mean UNHINGED.

Looking back, it seems now that the rehearsal and dinner on the evening before the great event were not unlike what took place in Napoleon's camp the night before Waterloo. Nothing had been left to chance. Nothing could prevent a victory on the coming day. Nobody would EVER forget this wedding. (*Just as nobody ever forgot Waterloo. For the same reason, as it turned out.*)

The juggernaut of fate rolled down the road, and the final hour came. Guests in formal attire packed the church. Enough candles were lit to bring daylight back to the evening. In the choir loft the orchestra gushed great music. And the mighty MOTB coasted down the aisle with the grandeur of an opera diva at a premier performance. Never did the mother of the bride take her seat with more satisfaction. She had done it. She glowed, beamed, smiled, and sighed.

The music softened, and nine—count them, nine—chiffon-draped bridesmaids lockstepped down the long aisle while the befrocked groom and his men marched stolidly into place.

Finally, oh so finally, the wedding march thundered from the orchestra. Here comes the bride. Preceded by four enthusiastic mini-princesses chunking flower petals, and two dwarfish ringbearers—one for each ring. The congregation rose and turned in anticipation.

Ah, the bride. She had been dressed for hours if not days. No adrenaline was left in her body. Left alone with her father in the reception hall of the church while the march of the maidens went on and on, she had walked along the tables laden with gourmet goodies and absentmindedly sampled first the little pink and yellow and green mints. Then she picked through the silver bowls of mixed nuts and ate the pecans. Followed by a cheeseball or two, some black olives, a handful of glazed almonds, a little sausage with a frilly toothpick stuck in it, a couple of shrimps blanketed in bacon, and a cracker piled with liver pâté. To wash this down—a glass of pink champagne. Her father gave it to her. To calm her nerves.

What you noticed as the bride stood in the doorway was not her dress, but her face. White. For what was coming down the aisle was a living grenade with the pin pulled out.

The bride threw up.

Just as she walked by her mother.

And by "threw up," I don't mean a polite little

ladylike *urp* into her handkerchief. She puked. There's just no nice word for it. I mean, she hosed the front of the chancel—hitting two bridesmaids, the groom, a ringbearer, and me.

I am quite sure of the details. We have it all on videotape. Three cameras' worth. The MOTB had thought of everything.

Having disgorged her hors d'oeuvres, champagne, and the last of her dignity, the bride went limp in her father's arms, while her groom sat down on the floor where he had been standing, too stunned to function. And the mother of the bride fainted, slumping over in rag-doll disarray.

We had a fire drill then and there at the front of the church that only the Marx Brothers could have topped. Groomsmen rushed about heroically, mini-princess flower girls squalled, bridesmaids sobbed, and people with weak stomachs headed for the exits. All the while, unaware, the orchestra played on. The bride had not only come, she was gone—into some other state of consciousness. The smell of fresh retch drifted across the church and mixed with the smell of guttering candles. Napoleon and Waterloo came back to mind.

Only two people were seen smiling. One was the mother of the groom. And the other was the father of the bride.

What did we do? Well, we went back to real life. Guests were invited to adjourn to the reception hall, though they did not eat or drink as much as they might have in different circumstances. The bride was consoled, cleaned up, fitted out with a bridemaid's dress, and hugged and kissed a lot by the revived groom. (*She'll always love him for that. When he said "for better or worse," he meant it.*) The cast was reassembled where we left off, a single flute played a quiet air, the words were spoken and the deed was done. Everybody cried, as people are supposed to do at weddings, mostly because the groom held the bride in his arms through the whole ceremony. And no groom ever kissed a bride more tenderly than he.

If one can hope for a wedding that it be memorable, then theirs was a raging success. NOBODY who was there will EVER forget it.

They lived as happily ever after as anyone does— happier than most, in fact. They have been married about twelve years now, and have three lively children.

But that's not the end of the story. The best part is still to come. On the tenth anniversary of this disastrous affair, a party was held. Three TV sets were mustered, a feast was laid, and best friends invited. (*Remember, there were three video cameras at the scene of the accident, so all three films were shown at once.*) The event was hilarious, especially with the running commentary and the stop-action stuff that is a little gross when seen one frame at a time. The part that got cheers and toasts was when the camera focused on the grin on the face of the father of the bride as he contemplates his wife as she is being revived.

The reason I say this is the best part is not because of the party. But because of who organized it. Of course. The infamous MOTB. The mother of the bride is still at it, but she's a lot looser these days. She not only forgave her husband and everybody else for their part in the debacle, she forgave herself. And nobody laughed harder at the film than she.

There's a word for what she has. Grace.

And that's why that same grinning man has been married to her for forty years. And why her daughter loves her still.

J OHN PIERPONT DIED A FAILURE. In 1866, at age eighty-one, he came to the end of his days as a government clerk in Washington, D.C., with a long string of personal defeats abrading his spirit.

Things began well enough. He graduated from Yale, which his grandfather had helped found, and chose education as his profession with some enthusiasm.

He was a failure at schoolteaching. He was too easy on his students. And so he turned to the legal world for training.

He was a failure as a lawyer. He was too generous to his clients and too concerned about justice to take the cases that brought good fees. The next career he took up was that of dry-goods merchant.

He was a failure as a businessman. He could not charge enough for his goods to make a profit, and was too liberal with credit. In the meantime he had been writing poetry, and though it was published, he didn't collect enough royalties to make a living.

He was a failure as a poet. And so he decided to become a minister, went off to Harvard Divinity School, was ordained as minister of the Hollis Street Church in Boston. But his position for Prohibition and against slavery got him crosswise with the influential members of his congregation and he was forced to resign.

He was a failure as a minister. Politics seemed a place where he could make some difference, and he was nominated as the Abolition party candidate for governor of Massachusetts. He lost. Undaunted, he ran for Congress under the banner of the Free Soil party. He lost.

He was a failure as a politician. The Civil War came along, and he volunteered as a chaplain of the 22nd Regiment of the Massachusetts Volunteers. Two weeks later he quit, having found the task too much of a strain on his health. He was seventy-six years old. He couldn't even make it as a chaplain.

Someone found him an obscure job in the back offices of the Treasury Department in Washington, and he finished out the last five years of his life as a menial file clerk. He wasn't very good at that, either. His heart was not in it.

John Pierpont died a failure. He had accomplished nothing he set out to do or be. There is a small memorial stone marking his grave in Mount Auburn Cemetery in Cambridge, Massachusetts. The words in the granite read: POET, PREACHER, PHILOSOPHER, PHILANTHROPIST.

From this distance in time, one might insist that he was not, in fact, a failure. His commitments to social justice, his desire to be a loving human being, his active engagement in the great issues of his times, and his faith in the power of the human mind—these are not failures. And much of what he thought of as defeat became success. Education was reformed, legal processes were improved, credit laws were changed, and, above all, slavery was abolished once and for all.

Why am I telling you this? It's not an uncommon story. Many nineteenth-century reformers had similar lives—similar failures and successes. In one very important sense, John Pierpont was not a failure. Every year, come December, we celebrate his success. We carry in our hearts and minds a lifelong memorial to him.

It's a song.

Not about Jesus or angels or even Santa Claus. It's a terribly simple song about the simple joy of whizzing through the cold white dark of wintersgloom in a sleigh pulled by one horse. And with the company of friends, laughing and singing all the way. No more. No less. "Jingle Bells." John Pierpont wrote "Jingle Bells."

To write a song that stands for the simplest joys, to write a song that three or four hundred million people around the world know—a song about something they've never done but can imagine—a song that every one of us, large and small, can hoot out the moment the chord is struck on the piano and the chord is struck in our spirit—well, that's not failure.

One snowy afternoon in deep winter, John Pierpont penned the lines as a small gift for his family and friends and congregation. And in doing so left behind a permanent gift for Christmas—the best kind—not the one under the tree, but the invisible, invincible one of joy.

(Postscript. In the winter of 1987, in the Methow Valley of the Cascade Mountains of Washington State, I finally got a long-held wish. The snow was three feet deep, the temperature hung at zero, the sky was clear, the sleigh was open, the horse was dappled gray with red harness and bells. And we dashed over the snow, laughing all the way.

Thanks, John Pierpont. Every word of the song is true.)

*I*F YOU ARE NOW OR HAVE EVER BEEN THE OWNER OF A dog, do not, I repeat, DO NOT read any further. Move on to the next chapter. Because if you do read what's coming, it will make you unhappy. And you will think ill of me, and you won't understand it, anyway. (Not everything in this book is for everybody, so trust me.)

If, however, you don't have a dog and don't want one, then we need to talk. What I am about to say speaks for a voiceless minority whose point of view never appears in the media. It is censored for fear of offending the dogworld.

I don't have any pets. None. Neither dog nor cat nor bird nor fish. Nevertheless, I am a reasonably responsible citizen, behave myself in public, pay my taxes, go to church sometimes, and am kind to children and old people alike. I love my family and they love me. But pets are not my thing. And I especially do not like dogs.

Once, at a large dinner party, I said that. Said I didn't like dogs. Said it a little louder than I intended, actually, but I really wasn't looking for trouble. I know the score on this subject.

The sudden silence made my ears ring. I could not have drawn more attention to myself if I had stood up on a chair and screamed "I HAVE RABIES!" Some of the people present give me a wide berth still.

Now, it is not a requirement that in order to be a good human being you must have a dog around the house. The Bible doesn't say, "Thou shalt keep dogs in thy abode to be blessed in My sight." The Book doesn't have much to say about pets, actually. Neither are dogs mentioned in the Declaration of Independence, the Magna Carta or the Declaration of the Rights of Man. You can go to heaven and be elected to public office without a dog.

(*Maybe not elected president, though. Do you notice that all presidents have a dog? There is always a First Dog. Or two or three. You have to have a dog to be president, I guess. I still love old Lyndon Johnson for picking up his beagles by their ears and swinging them around while the dogs bayed. "They love it—it's good for them," said Lyndon. I think he based his Asian policy on the same premises, but that's a touchy subject and I digress.*)

So what have I got against dogs? I'll explain.

First of all, for reasons I cannot explain, I have a congenital condition called "Pet Magnetism." Though I don't want to be near dogs, they are drawn to me with great force. The big ugly snarly biting ones go for me in a big way. And I can handle that. But all the rest of them seek me out as well. The wiggly tail-wagging slobbery ones want to be near my hands and face and lick and drool and breathe. I mind my own business, but they jump up on me and paw me and woof a lot. Uninvited. I swear it. I don't ask for any of this. And I don't do any of that to them, either.

Then there is the matter of doggy poo. I will avoid details except to say I seem to have a case of magnetism in this area as well. It happens so often I feel like going out into the world with Pampers on my shoes. I once collected a substantial bagful of the deposits left on my lawn by a neighbor's dog, and then carefully poured them out on his front porch. And he waded out into it in his house slippers to get his morning paper. He wasn't sure it was me who did it, but he kept his pooch off my lawn after that.

But enough on the subject. If you sympathize, I need not go on, and if you don't—well, more talk probably won't help.

Something else that doesn't need a lot of discussion is how people talk to dogs. I'm embarrassed by this. I really am. I wonder what the dogs must think.

Especially when people do this ventriloquist act where they speak to the dog and then answer for the dog in another voice. You know what I mean. You've heard it. Even dogs think it's weird. Watch a dog when a human does this. The dog can't believe what he's hearing, either. "Does Poochie wantum drinky? No, Poochie wantum go outside."

Do you know that we spend a couple of billion dollars a year on dog food alone in the USA? About twice as much as we do for baby food for people. Dog food accounts for about 11 percent of supermarket sales of dry groceries. The average supermarket chain devotes more than one hundred feet of shelf space to dog food and doggy needs. Doggy burgers and doggy bits and chicken à la dog and puppy yum-yums and all the rest of it. Take a look sometime. Seven and a half billion pounds total of pet food a year. And 40 percent of all dogs are seriously overweight—a vet I know told me so.

Add the cost of animals, breeders, veterinary care, medicines, and vitamins for dogs. Add the cost of accessories—collars, bowls, rhinestone leashes, sweaters, and doggy perfume. (*Yes, perfume.*) Plus the cost of beauty parlors, dog walkers, pooper-scoopers, and dog photography. Add it all together and Americans spend about seven billion dollars a year on dogs. Seven billion dollars.

Ninety percent of the dogs in the USA eat and live better than 75 percent of the people in this world.

And most of the dogs in America live and eat better than the 23 percent of the children in this country who live and eat below the official government poverty line.

Why is this? Why do we have all these dogs and treat them so well? Because we need protection from one another? Because we need some kind of love that humans can't give each other? Because we are bored or lonely or sentimental hunter/gatherers at heart, or what? My neighbor, who has two dogs, listens to my tirade in a patient way and tells me I just don't understand. I guess I don't.

The best feeling I have ever had about dogs came in a primitive Akah village in the mountains of northern Thailand. The Akah keep dogs like we keep pigs and chickens. They treat their cattle as useful working companions, give them names, and would never, ever think of eating one. But they eat dogs. They are not pets—dogs are simply food.

There are other ways to look at dogs.

*T*HE CARDBOARD BOX IS MARKED "THE GOOD STUFF." As I write, I can see the box where it is stored on a high shelf in my studio. I like being able to see it when I look up. The box contains those odds and ends of personal treasures that have survived many bouts of clean-it-out-and-throw-it-away that seize me from time to time. The box has passed through the screening done as I've moved from house to house and hauled stuff from attic to attic. A thief looking into the box would not take anything—he couldn't get a dime for any of it. But if the house ever catches on fire, the box goes with me when I run.

One of the keepsakes in the box is a small paper bag. Lunch size. Though the top is sealed with duct tape, staples, and several paper clips, there is a ragged rip in one side through which the contents may be seen.

This particular lunch sack has been in my care for

maybe fourteen years. But it really belongs to my daughter, Molly. Soon after she came of school age, she became an enthusiastic participant in packing the morning lunches for herself, her brothers, and me. Each bag got a share of sandwiches, apples, milk money, and sometimes a note or a treat. One morning Molly handed me two bags as I was about to leave. One regular lunch sack. And the one with the duct tape and staples and paper clips. "Why two bags?" "The other one is something else." "What's in it?" "Just some stuff—take it with you." Not wanting to hold court over the matter, I stuffed both sacks into my briefcase, kissed the child, and rushed off.

At midday, while hurriedly scarfing down my real lunch, I tore open Molly's bag and shook out the contents. Two hair ribbons, three small stones, a plastic dinosaur, a pencil stub, a tiny seashell, two animal crackers, a marble, a used lipstick, a small doll, two chocolate kisses, and thirteen pennies.

I smiled. How charming. Rising to hustle off to all the important business of the afternoon, I swept the desk clean—into the wastebasket—leftover lunch, Molly's junk, and all. There wasn't anything in there I needed.

That evening Molly came to stand beside me while I was reading the paper. "Where's my bag?" "What bag?" "You know, the one I gave you this morning." "I left it at the office, why?" "I forgot to put this note in it." She hands over the note. "Besides, I want it back?" "Why?" "Those are my things in the sack, Daddy, the ones I really like—I thought you might like to play with them, but now I want them back. You didn't lose the bag, did you, Daddy?" Tears puddled in her eyes. "Oh no, I just forgot to bring it home," I lied. "Bring it tomorrow, okay?" "Sure thing—don't worry." As she hugged my neck with relief, I unfolded the note that had not got into the sack: "I love you, Daddy."

Oh.

And also—uh-oh.

I looked long at the face of my child.

She was right—what was in that sack was "something else."

Molly had given me her treasures. All that a seven-year-old held dear. Love in a paper sack. And I had missed it. Not only missed it, but had thrown it in the wastebasket because "there wasn't anything in there I needed." Dear God.

It wasn't the first or the last time I felt my Daddy Permit was about to run out.

It was a long trip back to the office. But there was nothing else to be done. So I went. The pilgrimage of a penitent. Just ahead of the janitor, I picked up the wastebasket and poured the contents on my desk. I was sorting it all out when the janitor came in to do his chores. "Lose something?" "Yeah, my mind."

"It's probably in there, all right. What's it look like and I'll help you find it?" I started not to tell him. But I couldn't feel any more of a fool than I was already in fact, so I told him. He didn't laugh. He smiled. "I got kids, too." So the brotherhood of fools searched the trash and found the jewels and he smiled at me and I smiled at him. You are never alone in these things. Never.

After washing the mustard off the dinosaurs and spraying the whole thing with breath-freshener to kill the smell of onions, I carefully smoothed out the wadded ball of brown paper into a semifunctional bag and put the treasures inside and carried the whole thing home gingerly, like an injured kitten. The next evening I returned it to Molly, no questions asked, no explanations offered. The bag didn't look so good, but the stuff was all there and that's what counted. After dinner I asked her to tell me about the stuff in the sack, and so she took it all out a piece at a time and placed the objects in a row on the dining room table.

It took a long time to tell. Everything had a story, a memory, or was attached to dreams and imaginary friends. Fairies had brought some of the things. And I had given her the chocolate kisses, and she had kept them for when she needed them. I managed to say, "I see" very wisely several times in the telling. And as a matter of fact, I did see.

To my surprise, Molly gave the bag to me once

again several days later. Same ratty bag. Same stuff inside. I felt forgiven. And trusted. And loved. And a little more comfortable wearing the title of Father. Over several months the bag went with me from time to time. It was never clear to me why I did or did not get it on a given day. I began to think of it as the Daddy Prize and tried to be good the night before so I might be given it the next morning.

In time Molly turned her attention to other things . . . found other treasures . . . lost interest in the game . . . grew up. Something. Me? I was left holding the bag. She gave it to me one morning and never asked for its return. And so I have it still.

Sometimes I think of all the times in this sweet life when I must have missed the affection I was being given. A friend calls this "standing knee-deep in the river and dying of thirst."

So the worn paper sack is there in the box. Left over from a time when a child said, "Here—this is the best I've got. Take it—it's yours. Such as I have, give I to thee."

I missed it the first time. But it's my bag now.

"Young man, this tree is occupied." Voice from somewhere above me. Dismayed am I. As much by being called a young man as by having a tree I was about to climb turn out to be inhabited.

Dutifully returning to the ground, I peered up through the branches. Sure enough, there was an old lady up there. Way up there. White hair tied in a dark yellow bandanna, outfitted in blue jeans, sneakers, and leather gloves. An elderly tree spirit was settled into a high wide fork in this great elm. She wasn't coming down, either. "Find your own tree"— friendly but quite firmly. "Yes, ma'am."

Walked over to where a park workman was pruning bushes, but before I could ask he gave me my answer: "Yes, I know, there is an old lady up in that tree over there." He went on to explain that she was about sixty-five, retired, lives in an apartment down on Federal Avenue. Come spring and summer, she takes to the trees in the park. The workman thinks maybe she will have to be peeled out of her roost by the fire department someday, but in the meantime she seems to know what she's doing and doesn't bother anybody doing it. The lady just likes climbing trees.

I understand about that.

So much so that when I found out this month about the Tree Climbers International Club of Atlanta, Georgia, I became a dues-paying, card-carrying member. One of the reasons I joined is that they have a lot of safety equipment and a lot of techniques to share. I could sure use some.

Because recently I fell out of a tree. Crashing down through the branches, I scraped a good bit of skin off my elbows and gonged my head. Doctor declared it a concussion. Brain bruise. Along with some ego bruise as well.

"What were you doing up in a tree?" Doctor asked that. "Pruning it?"

(*Long pause. I think, That's what everybody is going to ask me. If I tell the truth, they won't understand. If I make something up, I won't understand.*)

"Umm," was my reply.

Climbing trees is my private pleasure, that's all.

But I'm not sure just why. It's more something to be done than talked about. Must be a primitive kind of thing—a comfort to the most ancient yearnings in my DNA. Ancestors spent several hundred thousand years up in trees. Which is why a comfortable seat in the crotch of an elderly elm feels so much like home. A rightness. A belonging.

And treehouses. They have the same rightness. All those rickety-board nests children lash and nail onto tree trunks up high where parents would not go except in their secret hearts. I would live in a treehouse if I could.

It's a little harder climbing trees now. Middle-aged men don't have the strength or the socially approved reasons. Pruning, yes. That's respectable work. Retrieving a cat or a kite, yes. Also respectable. But to play . . . or just to be there because it feels so lovely . . . well . . .

Being up in a tree is worth all the trouble, though. It's falling down out of a tree that is a loser. Especially if you bruise your brain. When I landed, I saw double for a while, which was interesting. Then I threw up, which is never interesting at all. Take the worst hangover feeling you ever had and double it—that's a concussion.

Doctor said to take it easy for a few days, which is fine with me—that's what I always try to do anyway.

And he said to stay out of trees, which shows you what doctors know about anything important to mental health.

Actually, falling is not so bad, either. It's a little like flying, but you don't have to flap your arms.

It's hitting the ground that is the hassle.

So the doctor should have said, "Try not to hit the ground." I could relate to that.

The problem is gravity. The reason you hit the ground is gravity. I know you know that, but I mention it because there is good news about gravity. It's easing up.

The moon is moving away from the earth at the rate of two inches a year, because gravity is decreasing. This means that every year you weigh about one potato chip less than you weighed the year before. It's true. And that means that the older you get, the softer you will hit the ground. Five hundred billion years from now, you could fall out of a really tall tree and never hit the ground at all. You would float and fly. Now *that's* something to look forward to. It's comforting to know there's hope for the future. Things are going to get better on some fronts, at least. I thought you'd like to know.

Anyway, I was back up in a tree today. Hair of the dog. And thinking that I wish more people spent more time up in trees, getting back to old places of well-being. Thinking about things. Old Buddha sat in front of one for a long time, and some pretty good ideas came to him. Wonder what he would have come up with if he had actually climbed up in it and sat down in its arms? . . .

If a whole lot more of us spent a whole lot more time up in trees, we might alter gravity in a different sense—the tendency of older folks to be grave—and lighten up. Imagine. You and me and a lot more like us way up in all the trees in the parks on a sunny April afternoon. Thinking. Waving to each other. Rock-a-bye-baby.

Want to join? Tree Climbers International, P.O. Box 5588, Atlanta, Georgia 30307, USA.

THE TEACHER IS QUIET. He is thinking, I can't believe I am doing this. He pulls on rubber gloves, reaches into a white plastic bag, and pulls out a human brain. A real human brain.

The students are quiet. They are thinking, I can't believe he is really doing this.

The students are thinking, If he hands it to me I will DIE, JUST DIE!

Sure enough, he hands it to them. They do not die.

When the brain comes back to him, the teacher tosses it across the table to the rubber-gloved quarterback of the football team, and he tosses it to his rubber-gloved tight end. Laughter as the tight end drops the brain on the table. The brain bounces.

To explain: In this beginning drawing class, I had been lecturing about the impact of brain research on the process of art, using pictures and diagrams and

anatomy charts. We had tossed around a cantaloupe
to get the feel of the size of a brain, but somehow
brains remained a bit abstract. The students had that
glazed expression on their faces that means this is
getting b-o-r-i-n-g.

In that moment of educational ennui, a freshman
girl says, "I can bring a human brain to school if you
want—my father has lots of them." (*Talk about a
full-scale class alert: "She's going to do WHAT?"*)

Well, it turns out her daddy is a bona fide research
neurosurgeon at the medical school and has jars and
jars of brains in his lab and he would be pleased to
have us see the real thing. So, sure, I can handle this.
"Bring a brain to school!" I shout at the departing
class. "ALL of you."

Sure enough, a week later, the freshman girl,
Queen Forever of Show-and-Tell, shows up with a
brain in a bag.

"Well, Mr. Fulghum, what do you think?"

If ever there was an appropriate use of the word
"nonplussed," it is now. This is what the students call
an "oooo-wow" moment of monumental propor-
tion.

"I have one of these things between my ears," I
said. It is made up entirely of raw meat at the
moment. It is fueled by yesterday's baloney sand-
wich, potato chips, and chocolate milk. And everything I am doing at the moment—everything I have

ever done or will do—passes through this lump. I made it; I own it. And it is the most mysterious thing on earth.

(*This brain in my hand wasn't raw, mind you—it had been preserved in formaldehyde. And no, it was not in fact icky or gross. Light beige in color, slightly damp, soft and rubbery, like clay. And just about the size of that cantaloupe we had passed around—only this one weighed almost three pounds.*)

"Now I can kind of understand the mechanical work of the brain—stimulating breathing, moving blood, directing protein traffic. It's all chemistry and electricity. A motor. I know about motors.

"But this three-pound raw-meat motor also contains all the limericks I know, a recipe for how to cook a turkey, the remembered smell of my junior-high locker room, all my sorrows, the ability to double-clutch a pickup truck, the face of my wife when she was young, formulas like $E = MC^2$, and $A^2 + B^2 = C^2$, the Prologue to Chaucer's *Canterbury Tales,* the sound of the first cry of my firstborn son, the cure for hiccups, the words to the fight song of St. Olaf's College, fifty years' worth of dreams, how to tie my shoes, the taste of cod-liver oil, an image of Van Gogh's "Sunflowers," and a working understanding of the Dewey Decimal System. It's all there in the MEAT.

"One cubic centimeter of brain contains ten billion

bits of information and it processes five thousand bits a second. And somehow it evolved over a zillion years from a molten ball of rock, Earth, which will itself fall into the sun someday and be no more. Why? How?

"*That's* what I think."

"Oooo-wow," chorus the students. The teacher is in a groove—got 'em.

Once again the brain is passed around from hand to hand, slowly and solemnly. Once again it is very quiet. The Mystery of Mysteries is present, and it includes us.

The single most powerful statement to come out of brain research in the last twenty-five years is this:

We are as different from one another on the inside of our heads as we appear to be different from one another on the outside of our heads.

Look around and see the infinite variety of human heads—skin, hair, age, ethnic characteristics, size, color, and shape. And know that on the inside such differences are even greater—what we know, how we learn, how we process information, what we remember and forget, our strategies for functioning and coping. Add to that the understanding that the "world" out "there" is as much a *projection* from inside our heads as it is a *perception,* and pretty soon you are up against the realization that it is a miracle that we communicate at all. It is almost unbelievable that we are dealing with the same reality. We operate on a kind of loose consensus about existence, at best.

From a practical point of view, day by day, this kind of information makes me a little more patient with the people I live with. I am less inclined to protest, "Why don't you see it the way I do?" and more inclined to say, "You see it *that* way? Holy cow! How amazing!"

This set me to thinking about Einstein's brain, which is somewhere in Missouri in a lab in a jar now. It was removed and studied to see if it was special in some way. (*No, it wasn't. It wasn't his equipment, but what he did with it, that cracked the window on the Mystery of Mysteries.*) When Big Al was in residence at the Institute for Advanced Studies at Princeton, a guest asked to be shown Einstein's laboratory. The great man smiled, held up his fountain pen, and pointed at his head. (*Oooo-wow*).

DO YOU KNOW ABOUT GEEK DANCING? (*No, that's not a mistake in spelling. Not Greek but GEEK dancing.*) Actually *geek* is in the dictionary. It refers to a carnival performer whose act consists of doing weird things. Biting the head off a live chicken, for example. In current slang, a geek is someone who looks like he might be capable of doing something like that. A person who bears watching. I hear young people using the word to describe anybody who is older and independent in lifestyle. There is a kind of compliment implied. It means you're a little strange, but interesting.

I guess it's true. A lot of us older types are a bit geeky. At some point your genetic code presses a switch in your head. You look in your closet to dress for the day and you say to yourself, who cares? You reach the point somewhere around sixty when you decide to just go ahead and weird out. You start out the door in your house slippers, headed for the grocery store, and you don't go back and change into shoes. To hell with it. Or you go out to the mailbox in your bathrobe—your oldest, sleaziest, comfiest bathrobe—and don't give a damn who sees you. Or when someone rings the doorbell, you don't check in the mirror to see how you look. You just open the door. It's their problem, whoever they are. So you aren't color-coordinated anymore. So? So you don't make your bed every day. So? Your life becomes like your old car—just as long as it runs and gets you there, who cares how it looks? Some people call this going to seed. Others call it the beginning of wisdom. Take your pick.

But I was going to talk about geek dancing.

When I get down and my life is logjammed and I need some affirmative action, I go where people dance. I don't mean joints where people go to get crocked and then wobble around on the floor to music. I mean places where people who really like to dance go to do that. I like dancers. Never met a serious dancer who wasn't a pretty fine human being. And I enjoy the never-ending pleasure of being surprised by just who dancers are. It does me good to see a couple of ill-builts—kind of fat and homely and solemn and all—get up on the floor and waltz like angels. When I see people like that on the street and start to look down my nose at them, a better voice in my head says "probably dancers" and I feel better about them. And me.

Anyhow. About geek dancing.

My favorite place, the Owl Tavern, has traditional jazz on Sunday nights from 6:30 to 9:30. The geek band plays swing music from Chicago and New Orleans from the good old days. Most of the people who show up are over forty, blue-collar one-beer types who have to be at work on Monday at 7:30. Not what you'd call a rowdy crowd. Dancers is what you'd call them.

I like to look around and find the king-hill champion geek for the evening. An old guy wearing invisible house slippers and his bathrobe. Balding, white hair, short, wrinkled. The kind who sort of lists to port when he walks. One who you might think was strictly nursing-home material if you saw him at a bus stop. But you see him here. And you know. A dancer. A dancing geek.

And he usually has his wife, the geekess, with him. A bit younger, always fluffed up a bit for dancing and has been for fifty years. Check her shoes. If they are black with mid-heels and a strap across the instep, it's a sure bet what she came for and what she is going to do.

The music cranks up, he takes her by the hand and kind of limps onto the floor. It's an act, just to set you up. And then it happens. She steps into a permanent spot formed by his embrace, the years fall away, and once again Cinderella and the Prince move to the music in the room and the music in their hearts. It takes about forty years to dance with a partner this way. Such ease, such grace, with all kinds of little moves that have been perfected without words. He dances flatfooted and with an economy of motion. She responds to unseen suggestions to twirl out and around and back. Their eyes meet from time to time, and you know that you're seeing a pretty happy marriage there on the floor. You'd have to love someone a long time to do what they're doing.

Sometimes the old geek asks another lady to dance. And somebody usually asks the geekess. They make whoever they are dancing with look pretty good. And feel pretty nice, too, I bet. An eighty-one-year-old geekess once asked me to dance on such an evening. I gave her my best, and she stayed right with me. "You are real good, honey," she said as I escorted her to her seat. I lived off that compliment for a week.

I want to be, and I fully intend to be, an old geek dancer. And my geekess and I are working on our dance routine. I realize that is a public responsibility: to help everybody stay as young as long as they can. To set good examples. And I don't want to die quietly in my bed, either—but at the end of the last dance some lovely night, sit down in a chair, smile, and pass on.

All this reminds me of something I heard about the Hopi Indians. They don't think there is much difference between praying and dancing—that both are necessary for a long life. The Hopis should know, I guess, as they have been through a lot and are still around. They say that to be a useful Hopi is to be one who has a quiet heart and takes part in all the dances. Yes.

OUR CHURCH HAD NOT HAD A FULL-BLOWN Christmas pageant in years. For one thing, we had become fairly rational and efficient about the season, content to let the Sunday School observe the event on their own turf in a low-key way. Then, too, there was the last time we had gone all out. That week of the Christmas pageant coincided with an outbreak of German measles, chicken pox, and the Hong Kong flu. The night of the pageant there was a sleet storm, a partial power failure that threw some people's clocks off, and one of the sheep hired for the occasion got diarrhea. That was about par for the course, since Joseph and two Wise Men upchucked during the performance and some little angels managed to both cry and wet their pants. To top if off, the choir of teenagers walking about in an irresponsible manner with lighted candles created more a feeling of the fear of fire and the wrath of God than a feeling of peace on earth. I don't think it was really all that bad, and maybe all those things didn't happen the same year, but a sufficient number of senior ladies in the church had had it up to here with the whole hoo-ha and tended to squelch any suggestion of another pageant. It was as if cholera had once again been among us and nobody wanted to go through that again.

But nostalgia is strong, and it addled the brains of those same senior ladies as they considered the pleas of the younger mothers who had not been through this ritual ordeal and would not be dissuaded. It was time their children had their chance.

And in short order, people who kept saying "I ought to know better" were right in there making angel costumes out of old bedsheets, cardboard, and chicken feathers. Just the right kind of bathrobes could not be found for the Wise Men, so some of the daddies went out and bought new ones and backed a pickup truck over them to age them a bit. One of the young mothers was pregnant, and it was made clear to her in loving terms that she was expected to come up with a real newborn child by early December. She vowed to try.

An angel choir was lashed into singing shape. A real manger with real straw was obtained. And while there was a consensus on leaving out live sheep this time, some enterprising soul managed to borrow two small goats for the evening. The real coup was renting a live donkey for the Mother Mary to ride in on. None of us had ever seen a live donkey ridden through a church chancel, and it seemed like such a fine thing to do at the time.

We made one concession to sanity, deciding to have the thing on a Sunday morning in the full light of day, so we could see what we were doing and nobody in the angel choir would get scared of the dark and cry or wet their pants. No candles, either. And no full rehearsal. These things are supposed to be a little hokey, anyhow, and nobody was about to go through the whole thing twice.

The great day came and everybody arrived at church. Husbands who were not known for regular attendance came—probably for the same reason they would be attracted to a nearby bus wreck.

It wasn't all that bad, really. At least, not early on. The goats did get loose in the parking lot and put on quite a rodeo with the shepherds. But we hooted out the carols with full voice, and the angel choir got through its first big number almost on key and in unison. The Star of Bethlehem was lit over the manger, and it came time for the entrance of Joseph and Mary, with Mary riding on the U-Haul donkey, carrying what later proved to be a Raggedy Andy doll (since the pregnant lady was overdue). It was the donkey that proved our undoing.

The donkey made two hesitant steps through the

door of the chancel, took a look at the whole scene, and seized up. Locked his legs, put his whole body in a cement condition well beyond rigor mortis, and the procession ground to a halt. Now there are things you might consider doing to a donkey in private to get it to move, but there is a limit to what you can do to a donkey in church on a Sunday morning in front of women and children. Jerking on his halter and some wicked kicking on the part of the Virgin Mary had no effect.

The president of the board of trustees, seated in the front row and dressed in his Sunday best, rose to the rescue. The floor of the chancel was polished cement. And so, with another man pulling at the halter, the president of the board crouched at the stern end of the donkey and pushed—slowly sliding the rigid beast across the floor, inch by stately inch. With progress being made, the choir director turned on the tape recorder, which blared forth a mighty chorus from the Mormon Tabernacle Choir accompanied by the Philadelphia Orchestra.

Just as the donkey and his mobilizers reached mid-church, the tape recorder blew a fuse and there was a sudden silence. And in that silence an exasperated voice came from the backside of the donkey. "MOVE YOUR ASS, YOU SON OF A BITCH!" Followed immediately by a voice from the rear of the church—the donkey pusher's wife—"Leon, shut your filthy mouth!" And that's when the donkey brayed. If we had held an election for jackass that day, there would have been several candidates mentioned. And the vote would have been pretty evenly distributed.

We are such fun to watch when we do what we do.

And though it has been several years since the church has held another Christmas pageant, we have not seen the last one. The memory of the laughter outlives the memory of the hassle. And hope—hope always makes us believe that *this* time, *this* year, we will get it right.

That's the whole deal with Christmas, I guess. It's just real life—only a lot more of it all at once than usual. And I suppose we will continue doing it all. Get frenzied and confused and frustrated and even mad. And also get excited and hopeful and quietly pleased. We will laugh and cry and pout and ponder. Get a little drunk and excessive. Hug and kiss and make a great mess. Spend too much. And somebody will always be there to upchuck or wet their pants. As always, we will sing only some of the verses and most of those off-key. We will do it again and again and again. We are the Christmas pageant—the whole damn thing.

And I think it's best to just let it happen. As at least one person I know can attest, getting pushy about it is trouble.

*P*ONDER. DID YOU EVER DO THAT? I've thought about that word ever since I came across it in the story of the birth of Jesus. "Mary pondered all these things in her heart" is what the Scriptures say. When you think about what the phrase "all these things" refers to, it's no wonder she pondered. Here's a teenage kid who has just had a baby in the back stall of a barn, with some confusion about just who the father is. Her husband is muttering about taxes and the fact that the head honcho in these parts, Herod, has opted for infanticide. And if that's not enough to think about, there's all this traffic of visiting astrologers, sheep ranchers, and angels, who keep dropping by with questions and proclamations and chorales. To top it off, the animals who are jammed in there with her *talk*. Not many cows speak Hebrew, but that seems to be what was going on. It certainly would give a person something to do some heavy thinking about.

I'd say "ponder" is the perfect word for what Mary was doing.

Old Job did a lot of similar thinking once upon a time there in his ash heap. And Jonah. Sitting in the steamy dark, awash in a whale's gastric juices and half-digested squid. Those guys did some pondering, too, I bet.

And me, too. I ponder. Annually, three or four days after the beginning of the new year. When there's nothing much special going on, which is why it is a special time. The first day when everything finally settles back into its normal routine state. The relatives have gone home. Christmas, too, has come and gone, and however it was—good, bad, or indifferent—it's over. New Year's Eve and New Year's Day are finished, and whether you whooped it up or just went to bed, that's all done. The holiday mess is cleaned up, the house has been tidied, and the leftovers have gone out with the garbage. It's too early to work on taxes, too soon to work in the garden.

It's not a totally down time. A Sunday afternoon walk in your neighborhood will tell you that life is moving on. A close look reveals the buds of another spring on the trees, and deep in their beds the daffodils and crocuses are feeling something moving in their toes. You know that because you feel vague stirrings in your own roots as well. And the days are already longer.

To ponder is not to brood or grieve or even meditate. It is to wonder at a deep level.

I wondered around for an afternoon this year on Ponder Day.

Wondering about the girls I used to love a long time ago. Where are they now? What are they like? Did I miss a good thing? What would happen if I tried to find them and called them up? (*"Hey, it's me!"* *"Who?"*)

I wondered about all those people who don't know it now, but who will not be here to ponder at this time next year. If they knew it now, would it help? And how about all those children who will be here this time next year, but who are just made up of parental desire at the moment?

I wondered about all the people in prisons—especially the ones who are unjustly punished—tortured. Do they have hope?

Somewhere along the way of Ponder Day wondering, I begin to make secret pacts with myself. The kind of thing you don't tell anybody because you don't want to be caught doing something dumb like making New Year's resolutions. You keep this stuff to yourself so you don't get caught out on a limb and then not do whatever it is you said you were going to do. (*I once listed all the good things I did over the past year, and then turned them into resolution form and backdated them. That was a good feeling.*)

As I pondered, I recalled high school days. Going back to school the first week after the winter holidays, swearing secretly to myself that I was going to do better this year. And for a few days I really did do better. I didn't always *keep* doing better—there are a lot of distractions when you are young—but for a few days at least—a few days of hopeful possibility—I had proof I really could do better. If I wanted to.

Now, in middle life, in thought that is more careful and vague and reflective of experience, I almost unconsciously promise myself the same. I could do better. The president and the pope and all the rest of humanity. We could do better.

I am reminded of a story I heard about a man who found the horse of the king and he didn't know it was the king's horse and he kept it, but the king found out and arrested him and was going to kill him for stealing the horse. The man tried to explain and said he would willingly take his punishment, but did the king know that he could teach the horse to talk and if so the king would be a pretty impressive king, what with a talking horse and all? So the king thinks what does he have to lose and says sure. He'll give him a year. Well, the man's friends think he is nuts. But the man says—well, who knows?—the king may die, I may die, the world may come to an end, the king may forget. But just maybe, just maybe, the *horse may talk*. One must believe that anything can happen.

Which is why, when asked where I had been, I told my wife, "Oh, talking to a horse." Gave her something to ponder.

"*W*ELL, SO, WHAT IS IT YOU DO?" Your basic strangers-on-a-plane question. Comes up at the PTA potluck and the corporate cocktail party and just about any other stand-around-and-make-small-talk situation you get into. It's a politely veiled status inquiry to clarify social standing. The bureaucratic version of the question is terse: Fill in the blank marked "Occupation." The Internal Revenue Service wants it that way—and the policeman giving you a ticket, and the passport agency, and the bank. Say what you are paid to do, and we will know who you are and how to deal with you.

When I ask people what they do, I usually get a stiff little piece of 3½″ x 2″ paper that summarizes their identity. Name, company name, title, address, lots of numbers—phone, telex, cable, and fax. Business card. If you don't have a business card these days, you are not to be taken too seriously. Though I sometimes think the truth may be vice versa.

For example, a fellow traveler's card said he was vice-president for systems analysis of Unico. "Well, so, what is it you really DO?" And he pointed at his title as if I had overlooked it. I asked again. "I mean, if I followed you around all day long, what would I see you doing?" He talked for a long time. I still do not really know what he does. And I am not sure he knows, either.

When it was my turn, I had no business card. Can't seem to get me down on that little piece of paper. What I do is kind of complicated and takes such a long time to explain that I often avoid the question and just pick something simple that's true but not the whole truth. Even this tactic has left me painted into difficult corners.

On an early-morning flight to San Francisco I told my seatmate that I was a janitor, thinking that she might not want to pursue that and would leave me to read my book. (*When I think of how I have spent my life and how much of it involves cleaning and straightening and hauling trash—I don't get paid for it, but that's what I do a lot.*) Anyhow, she was fascinated. Turned out she wrote a housewives' column for a small newspaper and was glad to spend the rest of the flight sharing her tips for tidy housekeeping with me. Now, I know more about getting spots and stains out of rugs than I ever hoped to know.

Turned out, too, that she was a member of the church where I was to speak on Sunday. I didn't know that until I stood up in the pulpit and saw her there in the third row. And it further turned out that she knew who I was all along, but was creative enough to think that if I wanted to go around on airplanes being a janitor, I probably had a reason.

Another time I was bumped into first class on a flight to Thailand and was seated next to a very distinguished-looking Sikh gentleman. Lots of expensive jewelry, fine clothes, gold teeth. (*Probably a high-caste bazaar merchant, I thought.*) When he asked me the what-do-you-do question I replied off the top of my head that I was a neurosurgeon. "How *wonderful*," said he with delight. "So am I!" And he was. A real one. It took a while to unscramble things, and we had a wonderful conversation all the way to Bangkok, but for ten seconds the temptation to be also deaf and dumb had been great.

Having learned my lesson, the next time I got on a plane and sat down next to someone who looked sympathetic, I told these stories and then suggested we play a game—just for the fun of it—and each make

up our occupation and pretend all the way to Chicago.
The guy went for it. So he declared he was a spy, and
I decided I'd be a nun. We had a hell of a time—one
of the great conversations of my life. He said he
couldn't wait until his wife asked him, "Well, dear,
how was your flight?" "There was this nun dressed in
a tweed suit . . ."

But it was the middle-aged couple from Green Bay
who had occupied the seats behind us who were
blown away. They had listened to the nun and the spy
in stunned silence. They *really* had something to say
when asked "How was your flight?" As the man
passed me in the concourse, he said, "Have a nice
day, Sister."

Filling in forms has led to similar situations. At my
bank I wrote "prince" in the blank for "Occupation"
on a loan application. Just that morning my wife had
said to me, "Fulghum, sometimes you are a real
prince." And sometimes I am. So, since I was feeling
princely, I put it in the blank. Clerk couldn't handle
it. And we had a friendly argument right there that is
at the heart of this matter of identity: Is my occupation
what I get paid money for, or is it something larger
and wider and richer—more a matter of what I am or
how I think about myself?

Making a living and having a life are not the same thing. Making a living and making a life that's worthwhile are not the same thing. Living *the* good life and living *a* good life are not the same thing. A job title doesn't even come close to answering the question "What do you do?"

Marcel Duchamp, whom most people think of as a fixture in the world of fine art during the period before 1940, was equally frustrated by the implications of the standard inquiry. He would answer, "I am a *respirateur*" (*a breather*). He explained that he did more breathing than anything else, and was very, very good at it, too. After that, people were usually afraid to ask him what else he did.

I know, I know. We can't go around handing out two-hundred-page autobiographies every time someone asks for minimal information. But suppose that instead of answering that question with what we do to get money, we replied with what we do that gives us great pleasure or makes us feel useful to the human enterprise? (*If you happen to get paid to do what you love, feel fortunate, but a lot of people don't.*)

Shift the scale a bit and answer the what-do-you-do question in terms of how you spend a normal twenty-four-hour day. I might say that I am a *sleepeur* and a *napeur*—one who sleeps and is very good at it. If ever there is an Olympic event for napping, I will go for the gold. Eight hours in twenty-four I am asleep in my bed, and every afternoon I take a thirty-minute nap. That is more than one third of my life. If I live to be seventy-five years old, I will have spent more than twenty-five years asleep. No other activity commands so much of my time in one place. While asleep, I cause no one else any pain or trouble, and it is an ecologically sound activity. If I got paid for how well I do it, I would be a very rich man indeed. It would be a better world if more people got more sleep, or at least spent more time in bed. There are people I don't much like when they are awake, but they don't bother me at all while they are sleeping, drooling into their pillows.

Had you asked me the do-be-do question today, I would have said I am a singer. Not only do I not get paid to sing, but in some cases friends might offer to pay me *not* to sing. Nevertheless, I love to do it. In the shower, driving to work, while I'm working, walking to lunch, and along with whatever I recognize on the radio. I sing. It is what I do. God did not put my desire together with the necessary equipment. My voice is what you might politely call "uncertain." I can hear the music in my head, but I cannot reproduce what I have heard, though it sounds fine to me. Over a lifetime of trying out for leads in musicals, I have always been told that I would be best in the chorus. And then got eliminated from the chorus because there were too many of whatever it is I am. I liked being a parent to my children when they were young and had no musical standards and would uncritically sing with me. It didn't matter that we didn't always know all the words or have the tune just right—we made it up. We singers are not thrown by technicalities. Singers are those who sing. Period.

Sometimes, when asked the what-do-you-do question, it occurs to me to say that I work for the government. I have a government job, essential to national security. *I am a citizen*. Like the Supreme Court judges, my job is for life, and the well-being of my country depends on me. It seems fair to think that I should be accountable for my record in office in the same way I expect accountability from those who seek elected office. I would like to be able to say that I can stand on my record and am proud of it.

"What I do" is literally "how I spend my time." As of this writing, in the fall of 1988, I figure in my life so far I have spent 35,000 hours eating, 30,000 hours in traffic getting from one place to another, 2,508 hours brushing my teeth, 870,000 hours just coping with odds and ends, filling out forms, mending, repairing, paying bills, getting dressed and undressed, reading papers, attending committee meetings, being sick, and all that kind of stuff. And 217,000 hours at work. There's not a whole lot left over when you get finished adding and subtracting. The good stuff has to be fitted in somewhere, or else the good stuff has to come at the very same time we do all the rest of the stuff.

Which is why I often say that I don't worry about the meaning *of* life—I can't handle that big stuff. What concerns me is the meaning *in* life—day by day, hour by hour, while I'm doing whatever it is that I do. What counts is not what I do, but how I think about myself while I'm doing it.

In truth, I have a business card now. Finally figured out what to put on it. One word. "Fulghum." That's my occupation. And when I give it away, it leads to fine conversations. What I do is to be the most Fulghum I can be. Which means being a son, father, husband, friend, singer, dancer, eater, breather, sleeper, janitor, dishwasher, bather, swimmer, runner, walker, artist, writer, painter, teacher, preacher, citizen, poet, counselor, neighbor, dreamer, wisher, laugher, traveler, pilgrim, and on and on and on.

I and you—we are infinite, rich, large, contradictory, living, breathing miracles—free human beings, children of God and the everlasting universe. That's what we do.

*I*N MOST AMERICAN HIGH SCHOOLS there is someone who teaches driver training. The top sergeant of automotive boot camp. Thankless task, a low-status job, about in the same league with the typing teacher as far as the faculty pecking order is concerned. The driver trainer is something of a nonperson. The parents of students never meet the DT; the faculty do not include him in their inner circle, and the students see the DT as a necessary evil. One more adult whose bottom they must kiss in order to get something they want. It's a job that anybody with half a brain could do—and anybody who wants the job doesn't have much ambition or talent or skill. Maybe.

Nevertheless, I would like to teach driver training for a while. It would be an honor, now that I see it the way Old Mr. Perry sees it. The students call him that. "Old Mr. Perry" (*not his real name*). They also call him "the Driving Master" and "Obi Wan Kenobi." Since the latter name refers to the Wise One in the Star Wars trilogy, I asked some students the reason, and they said to take a ride and see. So I did.

Jack Perry. Very average in appearance—not tall or short or fat or thin or old or young or straight or weird. Kind of generic. You wouldn't notice him on the street or pick him out of a police lineup for ever having done anything remarkable. Former navy chief petty officer, retired, one wife, four kids all grown, Protestant, tends his garden for pleasure. Likes cars and kids, so he's the driver trainer.

(It seems fair and useful to say that the conversation that follows is a reconstruction in my mind of what went on between us. What I am sharing is the spirit of the interchange. A taciturn man, Jack actually said much less than I am reporting, because he would begin a thought and then wave his hand and say, "You know the rest of that." I showed him this text and he said it was prettier than he actually talked, but he wouldn't disagree with it any. Part of why the kids like him is that he listens a whole lot more than he talks.)

—So you're the man who teaches Driver Training?
—Well, that's my job title, yes.
—I'd like to know what you really DO. The students say you are one of the really fine people around school—a "truly maximum dude," to quote one.

—You really want to know?

—I really want to know.

—Guess this sounds presumptuous, but I think of myself as a shaman—I help young men and women move through a rite of passage—and my job is getting them to think about this time in their lives.

Most of them are almost sixteen. They know a lot more about life and sex and alcohol and drugs and money than their parents or teachers give them credit for. And they are physically pretty much what they are going to be.

But we don't have any cultural rituals to acknowledge they're growing up. There's no ceremony, changing of clothes, or roles or public statement that says, This isn't a kid anymore—this is a young adult.

The only thing we do is give them a driver's license. Having a car means you move out of the backseat into the driver's seat. You aren't a passenger anymore. You're in charge. You can go where you want to go. You have power now. So that's what we talk about. The power.

—But what about actually learning to operate a vehicle?

—Oh, that comes easily enough—some driving time with suggestions—reading the manual—and they *want* it all enough to work on their own. But I don't talk much about that—they have to pass a test, and it usually takes care of itself.

—So what do you talk about when you're out driving?

—About their new power—opportunity—responsibility. About dreams and hopes and fears—about "someday" and "what if." I listen a lot, mostly. I'm not a parent or a schoolteacher or a neighbor or a shrink, and they hardly ever see me except when it's just the two of us out in a car cruising around. I'm safe to talk to. They tell me about love and money and plans, and they ask me what it was like when I was their age.

—Will you take me out for a ride? My driving could be improved.

And so we went. And so it was. My driving was improved—along with my sense of place and purpose.

This experience with the Driving Master emphasizes the profound truth of an old story. If you don't know it, it's time you heard it. If you know it, you ought to hear it again once in a while.

The story says that a traveler from Italy came to the French town of Chartres to see the great church that was being built there. Arriving at the end of the day, he went to the site just as the workmen were leaving for home. He asked one man, covered with dust, what he did there. The man replied that he was a stonemason. He spent his days carving rocks. Another man, when asked, said he was a glassblower who spent his days making slabs of colored glass. Still another workman replied that he was a blacksmith who pounded iron for a living.

Wandering into the deepening gloom of the unfinished edifice, the traveler came upon an older woman, armed with a broom, sweeping up the stone chips and wood shavings and glass shards from the day's work. "What are you doing?" he asked.

The woman paused, leaning on her broom, and looking up toward the high arches, replied, "Me? I'm building a cathedral for the Glory of Almighty God."

I've often thought about the people of Chartres. They began something they knew they would never see completed. They built for something larger than themselves. They had a magnificent vision.

For Jack Perry, it is the same. He will never see his students grow up. Few teachers do. But from where he is and with what he has, he serves a vision of how the world ought to be.

That old woman of Chartres was a spiritual ancestor of the man who teaches driver training, who is building a cathedral to the human enterprise in his own quiet way. From him the kids learn both to drive a car and drive a life—with care.

AFTER THE DISHES ARE WASHED and the sink rinsed out, there remains in the strainer at the bottom of the sink what I will call, momentarily, some "stuff." A rational, intelligent, objective person would say that this is simply a mixture of food particles too big to go down the drain, composed of bits of protein, carbo-hydrates, fat, and fiber. Dinner dandruff.

Furthermore, the person might add that not only was the material first sterilized by the high heat of cooking, but further sanitized by going through the detergent and hot water of the dishpan, and rinsed. No problem.

But any teenager who has been dragooned into washing dishes knows this explanation is a lie. That stuff in the bottom of the strainer is toxic waste—deadly poison—a danger to health. In other words, about as icky as icky gets.

One of the very few reasons I had any respect for

my mother when I was thirteen was because she would reach into the sink with her bare hands—BARE HANDS—and pick up that lethal gunk and drop it into the garbage. To top that, I saw her reach into the wet garbage bag and fish around in there looking for a lost teaspoon BAREHANDED—a kind of mad courage. She found the spoon in a clump of coffee grounds mixed with scrambled egg remains and the end of the vegetable soup. I almost passed out when she handed it to me to rinse off. No teenager who wanted to live would have touched that without being armed with gloves, a face mask, and stainless-steel tongs.

Once, in school, I came across the French word *ordure,* and when the teacher told me it meant "unspeakable filth" I knew exactly to what it referred. We had it every night. In the bottom of the sink.

When I reported my new word to my mother at dishwashing time, she gave me her my-son-the-idiot look and explained that the dinner I had just eaten was in just about the same condition in my stomach at the moment, rotting, and it hadn't even been washed and rinsed before it went down my drain. If she had given me a choice between that news and being hit across the head with a two-by-four, I would have gone for the board.

I lobbied long and hard for a disposal and an automatic dishwasher, knowing full well that they had been invented so that *nobody* would *ever* have to touch the gunk again.

Never mind what any parent or objective adult might tell me, I knew that the stuff in the sink drainer was lethal and septic. It would give you leprosy, or something worse. If you should ever accidentally touch it, you must never touch any other part of your body with your fingers until you had scalded and soaped and rinsed your hands. Even worse, I knew that the stuff could congeal and mush up and mutate into some living thing that would crawl out of the sink during the night and get loose in the house.

Why not just use rubber gloves, you ask? Oh, come on. Rubber gloves are for sissies. Besides, my mother used her bare hands, remember. My father never came closer than three feet to the sink in his life. My mother said he was lazy. But I knew that he knew what I knew about the gunk.

Once, after dinner, I said to him that I bet Jesus never had to wash dishes and clean the gunk out of the sink. He agreed. It was the only theological discussion we ever had.

My father, however, would take a plunger to the toilet when it was stopped up with even worse stuff. I wouldn't even go in the room when he did it. I didn't want to know.

But now. Now, I am a grown-up. And have been for some time. And I imagine making a speech to a high school graduating class. First, I would ask them, How many of you would like to be an adult, an independent, on-your-own citizen? All would raise their hands with some enthusiasm. And then I would give them this list of things that grown-ups do:

—clean the sink strainer
—plunge out the toilet
—clean up babies when they poop and pee
—wipe runny noses
—clean up the floor when the baby throws strained spinach
—clean ovens and grease traps and roasting pans
—empty the kitty box and scrape up the dog doo
—carry out the garbage
—pump out the bilges
—bury dead pets when they get run over in the street

I'd tell the graduates that when they can do these things, they will be adults. Some of the students might not want to go on at this point. But they may as well face the truth.

It can get even worse than the list suggests. My wife is a doctor, and I won't tell you what she tells me she has to do sometimes. I wish I didn't know. I feel ill at ease sometimes being around someone who does those things. And also proud.

A willingness to do your share of cleaning up the mess is a test. And taking out the garbage of this life is a condition of membership in community.

When you are a kid, you feel that if they really loved you, they wouldn't ever ask you to take out the garbage. When you join the ranks of the grown-ups, you take out the garbage because you love them. And by "them" I mean not only your own family, but the family of humankind.

The old cliché holds firm and true.

Being an adult *is* dirty work.

But someone has to do it.

*L*ADY I KNOW RUNS AN UPSCALE DOWNTOWN TOY store. Says her live-wire customers are mostly well-dressed middle-aged men who come in during the middle of the morning when their employees are back at the office working. In toy-store jargon these men are called "loose wallets." Only the best toys will do, and they never leave the store empty-handed. She says she can spot them coming down the street. They wear an eager, simpleminded look and walk with pleasant purpose, clearly coming to do something they enjoy. And they don't wait around for Christmas, either; they come any time of year.

Who are these big spenders?

Grandfathers. First-time grandfathers as often as not.

The answer to a toy salesperson's prayer.

And I am one. Which means I have been spending

a great deal of time in toy stores recently, shopping for dolls for my granddaughter.

(Fear not. I won't tell you all about my granddaughter. Because if you are not yet a grandparent, you really don't want to hear about this, and if you are already one, then all you want to do is tell me about your grandchild, who is, naturally, a more amazing kid than mine, and I don't want to hear about that.

This is the basic downside of grandparenthood. You want to talk about it a great deal. Nobody really wants to listen much to this illustrated lecture of yours—"Want to see some pictures?")

To continue. Dolls have changed since last I shopped for one twenty-five years ago. For one thing, most are "anatomically correct," and the salesperson is always eager to demonstrate this by holding up a dress or pulling down pants and exclaiming, "LOOK, THE REAL THING!"

This is the hardest part of doll shopping.

In theory, I am all in favor of this development, but I don't know which is more embarrassing—enduring the demonstration or asking not to be shown. I'll take their word for it. Perhaps the threat of the mandatory demo explains why grandfathers tend to shop for dolls in the middle of the morning when nobody else is in the toy store.

Toy manufacturers have progressed well beyond

realistic body parts. There's not much limit to what a doll can do.

"Baby Tickle" laughs when rubbed under her arms.

"Whoopsie" makes a shrieking sound and her hair flies up when her tummy is pressed.

"Baby Wet and Care" breaks out in a diaper rash. What's more, she comes not only with the lotion that clears up the rash, but with a lotion that gives her the rash in the first place.

Then there is "Newborn Baby," who comes "just as it is released from the hospital," which means it is life-size, wrinkly and soft and kind of ugly. Equipped with a hospital ID tag on its wrist, a pacifier, and—get this—a navel bandage where the umbilical cord was cut. It eats, drinks, whimpers, and messes its diapers (*it's anatomically correct, of course*) and spits up if you squeeze it. Comes in male, female, black, and white. (*No yellow or red. Why not?*)

This trend toward realism in dolls deserves applause.

It suggests a remedy for the population problem. Why not get *very* real about dolls?

How about "Baby Sick," who eats and throws up unexpectedly at the same time it develops diarrhea, and cries all night.

Or "Baby Disease," who periodically gets covered

with scabrous red spots, and coughs for three days and nights.

Or "Baby Difficult," who shouts "NO, NO, NO, NO!" instead of saying "Mama."

Or even "Baby Embarrassing"—you wind it up and it plays with its anatomically correct self while you are trying to change its diapers.

The ultimate baby doll would have ALL of these characteristics and actions. And whole generations of little girls and boys might grow up thinking very carefully about having real babies. They would know what they were getting into. Thus the doll manufacturers of America might become a powerful force in the service of population control.

Don't hold your breath while waiting for this development. The toy-store lady admits that the closer to being lifelike it is, the less likely a doll is to sell.

The "Newborn Baby Doll" I mentioned doesn't get any buyers even on sale at half price.

Even first-time grandfathers won't take it.

Especially not first-time grandfathers.

No, these guys buy exactly what you would expect: unblemished, unreal little beauties with fluffy dresses and ballerina features—the ones that are cute and sweet and soft. Without anatomical details, either, thank you.

Perfect is what they want.

Just like their granddaughters.

TALLY-HA, THE FOX! No, not tally-ho. Tally-ha.
Ha, as in "to laugh." This perversion of the traditional
incitement of the hounds is the rallying cry of the
Hunt Saboteurs Association of England. The HSA is
a troop of commoners who have taken an uncommon
interest in the ancient aristocratic sport of fox hunting.

Let us review. Hunting the fox involves gathering
some upper-crust sorts who wear funny clothes and
sit in skinny saddles mounted on rangy horses. At the
urging of a master of the hunt who is dressed in a red
sportcoat and who blows a brass horn, they all race
about the countryside over fences and hedges and
moor and hill and dale and field, all following after a
whole lot of dogs who are in turn chasing what they
hope is a fox. If it is a fox and the dogs catch it, they
tear it to pieces. All the horsy riders think of this as
great fun, as do the dogs, I suppose. What the horses
and fox think, I can only imagine. To belong to a

hunt club is to BELONG in a big way. The Royals are often right in the middle of all this, with a princess or a duke or two considered essential to the status of the hunt.

The newcomers to this jolly scene are the adherents of the Hunt Saboteur Association. More than two thousand enthusiasts dedicated to spoiling the fun. They are on the side of the fox. And against human cruelty to wild animals. They describe fox hunting as "the unbearable in pursuit of the uneatable."

Their goal is to bring chaos and embarrassment to fox hunting and to help a lot of foxes live happily ever after in one piece. To accomplish this, the Saboteurs are just slightly less organized than the Israeli Secret Service. No matter how discreet the hunt organizers try to be, the Saboteurs always seem to know their plans. Whenever a hunt is scheduled, the Saboteurs go into action. Here are just some of their tactics and activities:

Often they send out false or conflicting notices of hunt meetings for gatherings of riders at the wrong place on the wrong day.

Partisans hide in the woods and blow false horn signals to confuse riders, and sometimes they even mount up disguised as riders and rush about in the wrong direction.

On days before a hunt some of the Saboteurs range the fields and woods for miles around spraying artificial fox scent on trees and fences, and at the same time scattering juicy chunks of raw meat to distract the hounds.

The guerrillas have been known to set off village air-raid sirens and small smoke bombs to disconcert the riders, and even to set free all the horses while the riders are having a bite to eat and drink.

Recordings of fox barks and packs of dogs baying have been played to scatter the interest of dogs and riders alike.

Once, all the dogs in a pack were lured into a truck and driven miles and miles away.

The Saboteurs have crept into tack rooms and smeared honey on all the saddle seats, and even put red dye into all the watering troughs for miles around so the hunters would have to try to get their horses to drink what looks like blood.

Small tableaux have been staged on the commons in nearby villages—where men dressed up in fox costumes chase people dressed like aristocrats.

One plan is to fly overhead in a helicopter during a hunt, playing silly children's songs and tapes of silly laughter.

And I'm told that groups of Saboteurs have even run naked through the garden parties after the hunt—naked except for fake foxtails attached to their buns. And barking like dogs, of course.

Needless to say, the press is always notified of the

coming actions of the Saboteurs, and they love to come and record the whole affair. More than once the fox hunters have been made to appear both barbaric and foolish. All their names get published. Not good.

The hunt clubs don't like the Hunt Saboteur Association very much. But the hunters' deployment of police and lawyers only makes them seem more ludicrous, and spoils the hunt anyhow.

The result of all this is great fun for the SABs, as they call themselves, some great parties in the village pubs after their business is completed, and a diminishing interest in fox hunting for some of the hunters, as well as peace of mind on the part of not a few foxes.

I like the Hunt Saboteur Association. Not because saving foxes has a particularly high priority for me. And not just because I oppose any kind of cruelty. I applaud the spirit of the SABs.

So often doing good involves a kind of grimness. To assault evil, even small evil, with mischief, cleverness, merriment, and laughter—that takes genius few of us have but which, when it is found, graces the human scene and makes progress both possible and palatable.

If we could just figure out how to have more fun at it, maybe more of us would join the ranks of those who seek after justice and mercy.

WHAT I AM ABOUT TO SAY fits in someplace between the Ten Commandments and Murphy's Law.

God, you will recall, invited old Moses up on a tall
mountain out in the desert and handed him a couple
of solid-stone memos with some powerful words on
them. Commandments. God didn't say, "Here are
ten pretty good ideas, see what you think." Commandments. Do it or take the consequences.

Murphy, at the other extreme, was the ultimate
good-humored human cynic who said that no matter
what you do, it's probably not going to work out
very well anyhow. Some people think that Murphy
was an optimist.

As a middle ground, I offer Fulghum's Recommen-
dations. Items not touched on by God or Murphy,
really. And neither as ironclad as the first Ten or as
despairing as the endless variations on Murphy. Note

that there are only nine in my list I'm still working on the tenth. Or the eleventh, for that matter.

1. Buy lemonade from any kid who is selling.
2. Anytime you can vote on anything, vote.
3. Attend the twenty-fifth reunion of your high school class.
4. Choose having time over having money.
5. Always take the scenic route.
6. Give at least something to any beggar who asks.
7. And give money to all street musicians.
8. Always be someone's valentine.
9. When the circus comes to town, be there.

*T*HIS IS *1963*.

From deep in the canyoned aisles of a supermarket comes what sounds like a small-scale bus wreck followed by an air raid. If you followed the running box-boy armed with mop and broom, you would come upon a young father, his three-year-old son, an upturned shopping cart, and a good part of the pickles shelf—all in a heap on the floor.

The child, who sits on a plastic bag of ripe tomatoes, is experiencing what might nicely be described as "significant fluid loss." Tears, mixed with mucus from a runny nose, mixed with blood from a small forehead abrasion, mixed with saliva drooling from a mouth that is wide open and making a noise that would drive a dog under a bed. The kid has also wet his pants and will likely throw up before this little tragedy reaches bottom. He has that "stand back, here it comes" look of a child in a pre-*urp* condition.

The small lake of pickle juice surrounding the child doesn't make rescue any easier for the supermarket 911 squad arriving on the scene.

The child is not hurt. And the father has had some experience with the uselessness of the stop-crying-or-I'll-smack-you syndrome and has remained amazingly quiet and still in the face of the catastrophe.

The father is calm because he is thinking about running away from home. Now. Just walking away, getting into the car, driving away somewhere down South, changing his name, getting a job as a paper-boy or a cook in an all-night diner. Something—anything—that doesn't involve contact with three-year-olds.

Oh sure, someday he may find all this amusing, but in the most private part of his heart he is sorry he has children, sorry he married, sorry he grew up, and, above all, sorry that this particular son cannot be traded in for a model that works. He will not and cannot say these things to anybody, ever, but they are there and they are not funny.

The box-boy and the manager and the accumulated spectators are terribly sympathetic and consoling. Later, the father sits in his car in the parking lot holding the sobbing child in his arms until the child sleeps. He drives home and carries the child up to his crib and tucks him in. The father looks at the sleeping

child for a long time. The father does not run away
from home.

THIS IS *1976*.

Same man paces my living room, carelessly cursing
and weeping by turns. In his hand is what's left of a
letter that has been crumpled into a ball and then
uncrumpled again several times. The letter is from his
sixteen-year-old son (*same son*). The pride of his
father's eye—or was until today's mail.

The son says he hates him and never wants to see
him again. The son is going to run away from home.
Because of his terrible father. The son thinks the
father is a failure as a parent. The son thinks the father
is a jerk.

What the father thinks of the son right now is
somewhat incoherent, but it isn't nice.

Outside the house it is a lovely day, the first day of
spring. But inside the house it is more like *Apocalypse
Now*, the first day of one man's next stage of father-
ing. The old gray ghost of Oedipus has just stomped
through his life. Someday—some long day from
now—he may laugh about even this. For the moment
there is only anguish.

He really is a good man and a fine father. The
evidence of that is overwhelming. And the son is
quality goods as well. Just like his father, they say.

"Why did this happen to me?" the father shouts at the ceiling.

Well, he had a son. That's all it takes. And it doesn't do any good to explain about that right now. First you have to live through it. Wisdom comes later. Just have to stand there like a jackass in a hailstorm and take it.

THIS IS 1988.

Same man and same son. The son is twenty-eight now, married, with his own three-year-old son, home, career, and all the rest. The father is fifty.

Three mornings a week I see them out jogging together around 6:00 A.M. As they cross a busy street, I see the son look both ways, with a hand on his father's elbow to hold him back from the danger of oncoming cars, protecting him from harm. I hear them laughing as they run on up the hill into the morning. And when they sprint toward home, the son doesn't run ahead but runs alongside his father at his pace.

They love each other a lot. You can see it.

They are very care-full of each other—they have been through a lot together, but it's all right now.

One of their favorite stories is about once upon a time in a supermarket . . .

THIS IS NOW.

And this story is always. It's been lived thousands of times, over thousands of years, and literature is full of examples of tragic endings, including that of Oedipus. The sons leave, kick away and burn all bridges, never to be seen again. But sometimes (*more often than not, I suspect*) they come back in their own way and in their own time and take their own fathers in their arms. That ending is an old one, too. The father of the Prodigal Son could tell you.

MY SON IS A MOTHER. Grown up, married, first child. He and his wife have full-time careers and believe in Equal Rights and Equal Responsibility, in the spirit of New Parenthood. Son does his full share of everything for his daughter, and spends as much time with the child as his wife does. I call him a "mother" in that he does all those things that, once upon a time, mostly mothers did. He feeds, cleans and dresses, nurtures, accepts, approves, encourages, protects, comforts, and dearly loves the babe in his arms and heart. I admire him for this.

His daughter is just a year old. So far, so good. But since there are quite a few more laps to go, I thought I should give my son some advice about being a mother. Advice for him, not his wife. She knows what she's doing. And I have learned not to try to tell a woman how to mother. I have had some traumatic experiences along this line. I will explain.

For twenty-five years of my life, the second Sunday in May was trouble. Being the minister of a church, I was obliged in some way to address the subject of Mother's Day. It could not be avoided. I tried that. Mind you, the congregation was quite open-minded, actually, and gave me free rein in the pulpit. But when it came to the second Sunday in May, the expectations were summarized in these words of one of the more outspoken women in the church: "I'm bringing my MOTHER to church on MOTHER'S DAY, Reverend, and you can talk about anything you want. But it had better include MOTHER, and it had better be GOOD!"

She was joking—teasing me. She also meant it.

Year after year I tried to get it right. Somehow, having had a mother and having known quite a few firsthand didn't seem to count for much. I had never *been* a mother, so what did I know? I did give it my best—I swear. Tried to deliver on-the-one-hand-and-then-on-the-other-hand sorts of balanced, evasive sermons. Quoted a lot of big-name authorities, read sensitive poetry, avoided chancy jokes and gratuitous advice. But the Sunday never passed without half the congregation thinking I was a hypocrite for not laying it on the line about mothers, and the other half thinking I was an ingrate for not laying it on with a trowel as to how wonderful mothers really, eternally, are. What's a minister to do?

(*In passing, I note that Mother's Day has become an economic juggernaut. One hundred and forty million greeting cards are sold in the USA—very few humorous ones. And about seven billion dollars are spent for presents and taking Mom out to eat. Sixty million roses are given, not to count orchids and pot plants. Biggest commercial activity over a holiday after Christmas and Easter. And only at Christmastime does the telephone company do more business. There is fiscal power here not to be trifled with.*)

Around that second Sunday in May are focused other powerful forces—concentrated in memory and forever stored in hearts and minds and psyches. Serious stuff, too. Mother's Day is not noted for comedy.

One memorable Sunday I said that for all those who had wonderful mothers or who were wonderful mothers or who thought motherhood in general was just wonderful, I would like to say "WONDERFUL." But if this isn't you . . .

Then I gave a kind of moot quiz—asked some questions without asking for a show of hands.

1. How many of you find yourself involved in hypocrisy of the most uncomfortable kind around Mother's Day?

2. How many really don't like—or even really hate—
your mother, or hate being the mother you are?

3. How many really don't like or even really hate
your children?

4. How many don't really know your mother at all?

5. How many of you find Mother's Day painful,
especially when it involves thoughts and memories
of such matters as adoption, abortion, divorce,
suicide, rejection, alcoholism, alienation, abuse,
incest, sorrow, loss, and words like stepmother,
mother-in-law, and unspeakable obscene refer-
ences to motherhood?

I had other questions to ask, but the church had
become very quiet as I read my questions. The
congregation sat very still, and it was clear that a lot
more truth than they or I wanted to deal with was
among us. I stopped. Looked at them and they
looked at me. The look was pain. I sat down, not in
the pulpit chair but down in a pew where they were.
Enough had been asked to last a long time. There
wasn't much joy that Sunday in May. The cold
spring rain falling outside the windows of the church
didn't help much, either. Bringing up the whole
truth seemed like such a good idea at the time, but
now . . .

A visiting lady, who had "sainted mother" written
all over her face, accosted me after church: "Young

man, better men than you have gone straight to hell for suggesting less than what you said this morning. Shame, shame, SHAME for spoiling this day."

So. As I say, I'm a little gun-shy talking about Motherhood. Especially to women. As my own mother often explained when things did not go well: I was only trying to help.

My Sunday obligations are over now, and my mother is in her grave. I am on safer ground in passing some advice on to my son the mother. Advice for his older brother as well, who is engaged and has that fecund look about him that tells me motherhood is not far away from him, either.

For both my sons, then, some motherly thoughts from their father:

1. Children are not pets.
2. The life they actually live and the life you perceive them to be living is not the same life.
3. Don't take what your children do too personally.
4. Don't keep scorecards on them—a short memory is useful.
5. Dirt and mess are a breeding ground for well-being.
6. Stay out of their rooms after puberty.
7. Stay out of their friendships and love-life unless invited in.

8. Don't worry that they never listen to you; worry that they are always watching you.
9. Learn from them; they have much to teach you.
10. Love them long; let them go early.

Finally, a footnote. You will never really know what kind of parent you were or if you did it right or wrong. Never. And you will worry about this and them as long as you live. But when your children have children and you watch them do what they do, you will have part of an answer.

As I write this, Mother's Day is coming around again. I must remember to send my son some flowers and a card.

A FRIEND DOESN'T LIKE THE ESSAY "All I Really Need to Know I Learned in Kindergarten." Says it's nice as far as it goes, but it doesn't go far enough. Thinks it should go beyond "nice."

He's right. There are things I learned—and needed to learn—that were not taught in primary school. Teachers and adults would never tell you these things. Oh, they knew them all right, but they would never tell you they knew. You had to find them out for yourself or from your friends.

The ultimate source of this information was the snake in the Garden of Eden. I am talking about the forbidden fruit of the Tree of Knowledge. "Try it, you'll like it," whispered the snake. To eat of it is always trouble; not to eat is not to be fully human.

There are two parts to this body of knowledge: what I learned before I was thirteen, and what I know now. (*Some of these things I wanted to know. Some I did not. As my friend Lucy puts it, "Now that I am grown up, I sometimes wish I didn't know NOW what I didn't know THEN.")*

Sex. I learned that girls are different from boys; that there is a terrifying ecstasy in playing I'll Show You Mine If You'll Show Me Yours; that four-letter words about sex have awesome power, and if you write those words on walls, adults go crazy.

Crime. I learned how to take money out of my mother's purse, and how to get into and out of places I wasn't supposed to get into and out of—locked cupboards at home, and school buildings after hours.

And I learned that no matter what my mother said, sometimes you get away with it—you don't always get caught.

Furthermore, I learned to lie sometimes if I did get caught, because sometimes they would actually believe me. And if they didn't believe me, I could say I didn't know why I did it. Sometimes they believed that. But if the alibi didn't work and they punished me, it wasn't ever really as bad as they said it was going to be. And if I was going to have to suffer consequences anyhow, I might as well do some things that made it worth the trouble.

Remorseful crying afterward was useful—it broke their hearts.

God. No matter what they said, God is not watching you all the time. On the other hand, if you pray real hard, sometimes God will hear you and even make a deal with you. You may have to be good for a while to get what you want, but it may be worth it. (*I almost destroyed my third-grade teacher this way. I prayed for her to get sick and she did, over and over and over.*)

Power. Might may not make right somewhere in the world, but in our neighborhood the big boys always had the first and the last word. I learned that hitting people was sometimes necessary to bring people into line. Didn't my folks hit me? The basic rule is clear: Always hit someone smaller than you.

Skills. I learned how to spit between my teeth, how much fun it was to play with matches, how to play poker and cheat to win. I learned how to sneak out of my house, where to get a key duplicated, and how to drive the car up and down the driveway when my folks weren't home.

And Death. Not only did I discover that things could die, but I could kill them—bugs, lizards, worms, and mice. Old people died, but since I would never get old, I would never die.

What do I know now?

For one thing, the last item in the list is false. I did grow up to be old enough to know I, too, will die. I became one of those parents. My own children have themselves passed through kindergarten and their own back-alley education. Though my older son is a man now, only twenty-three years separate us, and we are both able to talk about our childhoods without total embarrassment. He KNOWS now—about the snake. He tells me all the rotten things he did behind my back when he was a kid, and I tell him all the things I knew he was doing but that I ignored because I didn't want to deal with the problem, considering what I had done at the same age.

Being a parent forces you into a benevolent hypocrisy. It goes with the job. It is comforting for the two of us to confess to each other—it clears the air between us and makes us people to each other.

Here's the tough part of what I know now: that the lessons of kindergarten are hard to practice if they don't apply to you. It's hard to share everything and play fair if you don't have anything to share and life is itself unjust. I think of the children of this earth who see the world through barbed wire, who live in a filthy rubbled mess not of their own making and that they can never clean up. They do not wash their hands before they eat. There is no water. Or soap. And some do not have hands to wash. They do not know about warm cookies and cold milk, only stale scraps and hunger. They have no blankie to wrap themselves in, and do not take naps because it is too dangerous to close their eyes.

Theirs is not the kindergarten of finger paint and nursery rhymes, but an X-rated school of harsh dailiness. Their teachers are not sweet women who care, but the indifferent instructors called Pain, Fear, and Misery. Like all children everywhere, they tell stories of monsters. Theirs are for real—what they have seen with their own eyes. In broad daylight. We do not want to know what they have learned.

But we know.

And it ain't kindergarten stuff.

The line between good and evil, hope and despair, does not divide the world between "us" and "them." It runs down the middle of every one of us.

I do not want to talk about what you understand about this world. I want to know what you will *do* about it. I do not want to know what you *hope*. I want to know what you will *work for*. I do not want your sympathy for the needs of humanity. I want your muscle. As the wagon driver said when they came to a long, hard hill, "Them that's going on with us, get out and push. Them that ain't, get out of the way."

"*S*IT STILL—JUST SIT STILL!" My mother's voice. Again and again. Teachers in school said it, too. And I, in my turn, have said it to my children and my students. Why do adults say this? Can't recall any child ever really sitting still just because some adults said to. That explains why several "sit stills" are followed by "SIT DOWN AND SHUT UP!" or "SHUT UP AND SIT DOWN!" My mother once used both versions back to back, and I, smart-mouth that I was, asked her just which she wanted me to do first—shut up or sit down? My mother gave me that look. The one that meant she knew she would go to jail if she killed me, but it just might be worth it. At such a moment an adult will say very softly, one syllable at a time: "Get—out—of—my—sight." Any kid with half a brain will get up and go. Then the parent will sit very still.

Sitting still can be powerful stuff, though. It is on

my mind as I write this on the first day of December
in 1988, the anniversary of a moment when someone
sat still and lit the fuse to social dynamite. On this day
in 1955, a forty-two-year-old woman was on her way
home from work. Getting on a public bus, she paid
her fare and sat down on the first vacant seat. It was
good to sit down—her feet were tired. As the bus
filled with passengers, the driver turned and told her
to give up her seat and move on back in the bus. She
sat still. The driver got up and shouted, "MOVE IT!"
She sat still. Passengers grumbled, cursed her, pushed
at her. Still she sat. So the driver got off the bus,
called the police, and they came to haul her off to jail
and into history.

Rosa Parks. Not an activist or a radical. Just a quiet,
conservative, churchgoing woman with a nice family
and a decent job as a seamstress. For all the eloquent
phrases that have been turned about her place in the
flow of history, she did not get on that bus looking
for trouble or trying to make a statement. Going
home was all she had in mind, like everybody else.
She was anchored to her seat by her own dignity.
Rosa Parks simply wasn't going to be a "nigger" for
anybody anymore. And all she knew to do was to sit
still.

There is a sacred simplicity in not doing something—
and not doing it well. All the great religious leaders

have done it. The Buddha sat still under a tree. Jesus sat still in a garden. Muhammad sat still in a cave. And Gandhi and King and thousands of others have brought sitting still to perfection as a powerful tool of social change. Passive resistance, meditation, prayer—one and the same.

It works even with little kids. Instead of telling them to sit still, you yourself can sit very still and quiet. Before long they will pay a great deal of attention to you. Students in class are also thrown by silent stillness on the part of a teacher. It is sometimes taken for great wisdom.

And sitting still works with grown-ups. On the very same bus route Rosa Parks used to travel, anybody can sit anywhere on the buses now, and some of the drivers are black—both men and women. The street where she was pulled off the bus has been renamed: Rosa Parks Avenue.

A new religion could be founded on this one sacrament. To belong would be simple. You wouldn't have to congregate on a special day in a special place. No hymns, no dues, no creeds, no preachers, and no potluck suppers. All you have to do is sit still. Once a day, for fifteen minutes, sit down, shut up, and be still. Like your mother told you. Amazing things might happen if enough people did this on a regular basis. Every chair, park bench, and sofa would become a church.

Rosa Parks is in her seventies now, doing most of her sitting in a rocking chair, living in quiet retirement with her family in Detroit. The memorials to her sitting still are countless, but the best ones are the living tributes in the form of millions of people of every color getting on thousands of buses every evening, sitting down, and riding home in peace.

If there is indeed a heaven, then I've no doubt that Rosa Parks will go there. I imagine the moment when she signs in with the angel at the pearly gates.

"Ah, Rosa Parks, we've been expecting you. Make yourself at home—take any seat in the house."

WHAT I'M ABOUT TO SAY ABOUT BLOOD begins with bagels. A bagel will not fit gracefully into an electric toaster. Or if it goes in, it will not come out—unless you employ a screwdriver. This postulate has been completely tested. Recently. So you have to cut the bagel in half, sliced horizontally—the hard way. This also cannot be accomplished gracefully. A very sharp butcher knife and a pair of pliers helps. But not very much. If you want to slice off a piece of your finger, this is an ideal setup.

The normal tendency when you slice your finger is to want to call Medic One. Blood equals emergency. But if you can somehow wire around your panic, an existential moment may come if you stand still and bleed a little into the sink. You will not die of this cut—you've cut your finger before. (And there are no Band-Aids in the Band-Aid box in the linen closet, anyway. The children used them to wrap Christmas presents when the Scotch tape ran out.) Calm down. Go ahead and breathe. And bleed.

See, you won't bleed long. Your own interior Medic One takes care of the problem in an amazing way. In the meanwhile, there's the most beautiful color in the sink. A scarlet red you can't buy in a tube at the art-supply store. And it's homemade. The closest thing to it outside your body is seawater. When we came up out of the sea we internalized it. There's about five quarts of this stuff inside us, and if you take a pint out and give it away, you make a replacement pint in no time at all—without even thinking about it. You just cook up some more blood.

Like a lot of other things about us, the more we study blood, the more fantastic and mysterious and wondrous it becomes. It's 55 percent liquid and 45 percent solids—red cells and white cells and platelets. There are twenty-five trillion red cells alone; fastened end to end they would form a string that would wrap around the earth three times. This blood moves through sixty thousand miles of vessels in your body, regulates your temperature, and moves energy and minerals and hormones and chemicals to the right place with an efficiency envied by all public utilities, including the garbage-collection company.

You've stopped bleeding now. A sixteen-step protein cascade effect has built a dam and shut off the flow. At the point of injury, white cells have gathered to fight infection, other blood elements have already brought repair materials, and healing has begun. Endorphins have been supplied to curtail pain—it doesn't really hurt.

If you'll just stand there patiently for five minutes these things will happen.

Without your thinking or planning or organizing or trying.

It's very beautiful, this blood of yours.

It's very powerful and efficient.

It's worthy of respect.

It is life.

Confirmed.

(I should point out that if, in the midst of this epiphany, some member of your family should walk in and see the bloody bagel and the knife and the general mess and shambles of the kitchen, and the toaster plugged with smoking bread dough, and you staring glassy-eyed into the sink, you may have some explaining to do. So, explain. When the student appears, the teacher is prepared.)

"*A*SPIRIN. WE DON'T KNOW EVERYTHING ABOUT how it works. We know what it does, but we don't know how." So said a medical researcher to me during the making-small-talk part of a dinner party. Wait a minute. This guy is a Ph.D. and an M.D. and has government grant money running out his pockets, and he doesn't know about aspirin? This is not small talk. But it's true. He doesn't know—nobody else knows—not even the guy in the TV ad dressed up to look like a doctor. Big mystery, which has been around for a long time. Chinese doctors prescribed it a thousand years ago. "Chew up some willow bark and call me in the morning" is what they said back then. Willow bark has acetylsalicylic acid in it. That's aspirin, which is easier to pronounce and easier to get down your gullet than willow bark.

There's some comfort in knowing that the Ph.D. and M.D. types are thrown by something so common

and simple as aspirin. Mystery remains as close at
hand as my medicine cabinet.

In my working journal there is an old list under the
heading: "Ordinary Things We Don't Know About."
The list got started when I read a statement in some
science magazine to the effect that "we don't know
how water moves from the ground up through the
trunk and out to the leaves of a tree." Amazing! I
thought we had trees figured out.

So I started the list. Every time I read of an expert
saying we don't know about this very simple ordinary
thing or another, it went on my list.

Homing pigeons came next. Then the common
cold. Followed by hair loss. But when I read about
Heisenberg's Principle of Uncertainty in a physics
course, I realized my list was a fool's task. Electrons are
everywhere, and we not only *don't* know if they are a
wave or a particle, we *can't* know. If electrons are a
problem, well, everything is.

So I began a new list. "Signs of the Cosmic Glitch"
is the heading. The information about electrons
pointed at a basic untidiness. Example: The earth
wobbles seventy-two feet off center. Like a top
spinning on its axis somewhat cockeyed. Right this
very minute we are all wobbling just a little. If you
ever feel kind of queasy for no particular reason, it
may be the wobble.

Now. We learned that the earth is slowing down,

so we have to mess with the clocks and throw in a leap-year from time to time—and we know why this is. But the wobble? Lots of theories, but nobody can explain it. Cosmic Glitch.

Science has tended to dismiss such matters as being in the range of permissible error. In almost all research in almost every field, there has always been some persistent little inconsistency. The Glitch. And it has always been easier to build it into an equation and discount it rather than try to explain it.

It's like knowing that no matter how carefully and long you may stir your hot breakfast cereal, there will always be at least one small lump of dried, uncooked cereal hiding somewhere in the mix. After a few years you learn to expect and accept the lump and assume it just goes with the territory. But the WHY is the interesting part, as it turns out.

For suddenly science has become very interested in the behavior of your breakfast cereal. This pattern that always seems to include the unmixed lump has become the business of something called "Chaos Science," the most important shift in scientific thinking since Einstein's little formula.

Chaos Science is the study of the Cosmic Glitch. And the Glitch is in every field of science and every realm of experience. Chaos Science suggests that the problem has not been one of small errors, but one of larger information. The pattern of existence turns out to be far more complex and complicated than we thought—on every level.

Chaos Science has led researchers back to the most fundamental everyday matters—the formation of clouds, the mixing of paint, the flow of traffic, the spread of disease, and the freezing of water in pipes. The cycles of earthquakes and the eruption of volcanos fits into Chaos Science, too, which is pretty important these days if you live in California or in the Cascade Mountains. The problem of the larger pattern pervades every activity we know of.

The language being used to label the new fields of study is itself appropriately glitchy. When I attended the 155th national meeting of the American Association for the Advancement of Science, in San Francisco, I heard discussions in the field of Chaos Science about such topics as "fractal fingering," "strange attractors," "dangling bond defects," "folded-towel diffeomorphisms," "Eden growth," "smooth noodle maps," and "lattice animals." There's more poetry and metaphor in Chaos Science, and I think it's because we're talking about something so far out on the edge that even though we sense a mighty truth, we don't have language symbols to accurately nail down what we sense.

So we call it Chaos Science. By "Chaos" we mean simply what we can't understand.

It's as if we were the most numerous and oldest and

most established ant colony in Chicago. And every once in a while, some of the most brilliant ants wander out together and take a look at Chicago—or what they can see of it. The farther away from the ant heap they get, the more mysterious things seem to be. Recently they happened to be standing alongside a formerly quiet area in their universe when there was a mighty tremor, a huge darkness, and a mighty blast of wind. They had not predicted such activity. They sensed something unimaginable was going on. And reported a new condition of the universe when they returned to the anthill—something that would force a revision of their understanding. Some wanted to call this Chaos. Some wanted to call it the Mysterium Tremendum. Others, the Backfire of the Big Bang. The Wrath of God was also suggested. A new science—a new chapter in the Great Book of the Way It Is. Little did they know that they had happened onto a seldom-used railroad siding when a freight train passed by.

The bad news is that the ants will never ever comprehend Chicago. The good news is that they sense they are right in the middle of something infinitely wonderful and the more they try to understand it, the more amazing it seems to be. Seems to be in the nature of the ants to keep going out and pushing the limits of the known until they come to a new edge. Naming what's beyond seems to help accommodate that which cannot be understood. It is the ants' way.

Chaos Science is the study of process—that which won't hold still. The study of that which is still becoming, rather than of what is.

Chaos Science is my kind of science. I like knowing that no matter what, there is this cosmic untidiness— an unexplainable hiccup in the order we think we perceive, an unpredictability, a mutational inclination, a glitch in the works that anchors mystery and wonder to the center of being. And that the aspirin I hold in my hand and the clouds overhead remain as mysterious to the experts as to me.

Chaos. I can relate to that. My life is chaos most of the time. I am in tune with the universe. It feels like home.

"*T*HE GREAT HUGGING PLAGUE*" is how it's remembered now. Broke out in our church in the seventies—
back in the days when loving everybody was the way
to straighten the world out once and for all. The
Sunday Morning Greeters Group started it. They
decided to hug every single person who walked in the
front door. Wanted to make everyone feel loved and
welcome right away. They were just going to try it
for a couple of Sundays and see how it went. But
things got a little out of hand.

Sometimes as many as six people were standing
around the vestibule of the church on a Sunday
morning waiting to hug anything that was moving.
The Greeters Group even started wearing signs
around their neck that said things like: DESIGNATED
HUGGER, HUGGER AT LARGE, HUG ME, I'M HUMAN, and
GOD LOVES A CHEERFUL HUGGER. They thought a little

touch of levity would grease the wheels of social interchange and make hugging really happen.

As I say, it got out of hand. It was said that when business was slow, the huggers hugged each other for practice. Some hugged a chair or two, and even the janitor got hugged as he tried to clean up some spilled coffee. A stray dog strolled in and got hugged, as did several people who were looking for the Methodist church nearby and wandered in by accident. I heard that someone even hugged the coffee urn—it was warm and made comforting sounds, so he hugged it. There was a rumor that some parishioners just came to be hugged, and went home without going to church. Hugging junkies. It became an epidemic. The great hugging plague.

Not everybody wanted to be hugged. A somewhat quiet and reserved member of the congregation wrote a letter to me and the board of trustees. Said he had developed a hugging aversion. Said he didn't want to keep other people from doing it, but he was nervous about getting assaulted by joy when he came to church. He had tried sneaking in through the kitchen door, but one of the cooks had got caught up in the mania and not only hugged him but spilled chicken bouillon on his suit in the process. Said his glasses got knocked off and his toes stepped on in the morning melee, and he felt social pressure—if he capitulated to one hugger, he'd have to hug everyone else, too. Said he was anxious about going to the rest room when huggers were in there.

But he didn't just complain. He had some constructive suggestions. Perhaps a second entrance for people who just wanted to say "hi" or shake hands when they came to church. Maybe a medic-alert tag to wear—one with a silhouette of people hugging and a red line across it.

Furthermore, he suggested organizing a group to be called HA!—Huggers Anonymous—for those who wanted to kick the habit. Perhaps, he suggested, we could offer T-shirts that said: DON'T HUG ON ME or UNTOUCHABLE or UNCLEAN or something.

He said the only way he had been able to put off the huggers was to walk through the door with his thumb in his mouth. The huggers didn't quite know how to handle that. He had thought of carrying an open umbrella or a small child with a runny nose.

It was while the board and I were working out a response to this concern that the first wave of free-wheeling kissing hit. Seems that somebody had been down to visit the Episcopal church and there was this exercise called the Kiss of Peace, where you held hands, sang the benediction, and then turned and kissed people on the cheek. Great idea! So our huggers were all for expanding the action and doing some handholding and peacekissing at the end of the service. Sure enough, they tried it one Sunday morning without any warning. Well, it was a Sunday to remember, let me tell you. Guess we weren't quite ready for unprovoked kissing, for the sake of peace or anything else.

The board of trustees talked about hugging and kissing a great deal more than they ever intended. It made trying to deal with a leaky chancel roof seem simple in comparison. And I felt the need to address the whole issue of public affection in one of those wishy-washy on-the-one-hand-and-then-on-the-other-hand sermons that left me as confused as the congregation. Aagghh.

The seventies have come and gone. Aggressive affection is out of fashion. People in that church still hug each other, but they are more careful about it now. The shift is important to recognize. The purpose of hugging has changed. Where once it was a statement about the liberation of the hugger, it is now a statement of caring about the huggee. A shift from getting to giving. A shift from Look at Me to I Am Seeing You. A shift from knowing What I Want to noticing What Someone Else Needs. You might not learn this just from watching two people hug each other. You'd have to put your arms around somebody to understand.

"*T*HEY LIED TO ME ABOUT THANKSGIVING!" A former student of mine complains by phone from college, where she is getting the latest revisionist view of American history. Up until high school she had been deeply committed to the Thanksgiving story as reenacted by her fifth-grade class.

She played Pocahontas, the ravishingly beautiful Indian princess, in a floor-length velour nightgown, and got to marry the tall handsome blond kid playing Miles Standish. He looked magnificent in the big black cardboard hat, sneakers spray-painted silver, and a curly black mustache leftover from the melodrama the class produced in October. Furthermore, he was armed with a plastic submachine gun, which gave the pageant a measure of tension, seeing as it was really a watergun loaded with cranberry juice.

In this fifth-grade version of the story of our foremothers and forefathers, the Pilgrims sat down at a long row of card tables across from the Indians. You could tell the Indians by the turkey feathers in their hair and the lipstick smeared on their faces and arms. Everybody bowed their heads for the Great Prayer of Thanksgiving and then ate cold turkey sandwiches washed down with root beer. They sang "Home on the Range," that old hymn of thanksgiving, followed by ice-cream bars and licorice whips. Then they all went out for recess and the Pilgrims beat the hell out of the Indians in a game of Red Rover.

That was the beginning of Thanksgiving as we know it today. The fifth-grade class could believe in this and be pretty appropriately thankful about the whole deal.

Ah, but in high school my young friend was told that, no, it wasn't like that at all. Pilgrims were pretty uptight, right-wing prudes—fascistic bigots who were not only harsh on the Indians but harsh on each other as well. Pilgrims were against fun and spent most of their spare time in church, where they didn't even sing. Sometimes they burned people for being witches. They were against science, education, dancing, chocolate, tobacco, and fooling around between girls and boys. No radio, no TV, no rock 'n' roll, no drive-ins. Just church and hard work. My young friend loathed these Pilgrims and had refused to eat Thanksgiving dinner one year in protest against her parents' celebration of evil incarnate.

But now she is in college and it is 1988 and she is outraged by all the lies she has been told. She knows now that the Pilgrims did not dress in black all the time; they did not come to found America; and they were not communists or fascists, but rebels who ran away from home so they could go to church how and when and where they wanted to. (*Just like my young friend.*) They drank wine, ate good food when they had it, smoked tobacco, had sex . . . and young Puritans got to lie in bed together with their clothes on with a board between them—"bundling"—and any teenager could get around that. Then the Pilgrims built Harvard University, where my young friend is now, and where all those fine Pilgrim traditions are continued to this day. (*"We don't use a board in bed now, though,"* says she.)

Furthermore, the Pilgrims did not celebrate Thanksgiving Day and did not pray some great prayer. All they did was EAT their bellies full because they were so hungry. And none of their relatives dropped in from out of town, either; the Pilgrims came to get *away* from their relatives—the ones in England who wanted them to go to the right church. My young friend can relate to this version of the Pilgrims—they were her kind of guys.

Oh yes, and about the Indians—they don't celebrate Thanksgiving, either. Once was enough, actually. Ever since they had lunch with the Pilgrims, they've had nothing but trouble and not enough to eat. My young friend is taking a course in Native American culture, a trendy class that turns out fledgling shamans each term.

This is but a short summary of a much longer telephone call on Thanksgiving Day. Mostly she was lonely back there in New England. Like the Pilgrims once, I suppose.

Talking to college students is always instructive— nice to know what the younger generation is stirred up about. It's true that history is confusing. And my young friend will encounter several more versions of the Thanksgiving story and all the rest of the human story before the picture begins to clear. Her feeling that the Pilgrims were a lot like her is progress. I suspect they were.

And me—well, my version is that whatever happened on that autumn day in 1621, what went through the minds of the Pilgrims that night as they laid them down to sleep was not too different from what goes through mine each year at the feast's end:

"Dear God, I'm glad that's over . . . we all ate too much again . . . but nobody got hurt . . . now it is quiet and we are all warm and dry and have a nice place to sleep . . . life goes on . . . and for now, that is not only enough, it is pretty fine . . . and I, for one . . . give thanks."

A UNITARIAN MINISTER IS OFTEN ASKED to perform interfaith marriages. "Mixed marriage" is the common term. But widely differing religious backgrounds are not usually all that's involved. Any wedding wherein the bride or groom is marrying someone outside the family borders of race or class is "mixed." To be asked to perform such a marriage is to join two people trying to cross a mine field without getting blown apart.

The paradigm is the wedding of a very lovely young woman from Brooklyn. Huge family. Polish immigrant stock. And Jewish. Her tall, dark, and handsome fiancé hailed from Detroit. Likewise a huge family. Likewise immigrant stock, but Irish. And Roman Catholic. The bride's family included a rabbi and a cantor; the other team had some priests and a nun on the roster. It was bad enough that the young man and woman had come all the way out

West to Seattle to attend graduate school; bad enough that they might not marry someone from the old neighborhood; but to fall in love with and, even worse, MARRY someone "not like us" was a shameful disaster—a familial earthquake of the first magnitude. Unthinkable.

But Ms. Brooklyn and Mr. Detroit were twenty-one years old and overwhelmed with Love. And Love, they were quite certain, could find a way through any obstacle. The minister had his doubts, having a few shrapnel wounds on his soul from having not made it through mine fields with such couples before.

Now from here on out in this story—almost to the very end—the pieces of the plot fall like dominoes. So predictably did it go that I could have made money on side bets as to what was going to happen next. I could have told them, but they wouldn't have listened. Sometimes people have to find out things for themselves. Here's how they saw their options:

Plan A: Get married by a judge and never tell the folks back East. But—and here comes Love again—they really loved their parents and if their parents found out, which they were bound to, they would be deeply wounded, especially when they found out there hadn't been a religious ceremony of *some* kind. And so—

Plan B: Get married by a Unitarian minister and tell

the parents a day later. A kind of semi-elopement. The parents had no idea what Unitarians believed, but at least it was a religious deal and in a church. Good idea. Enter the Reverend Mr. Fulghum. Which led to—

Plan C: As long as the wedding was going to be in a church with a minister, they might as well invite just a few friends instead of having only two witnesses. And as long as they were inviting those few friends, they might as well invite a few more friends, since they didn't want to hurt anybody's feelings. And since they were now at the soft edge of the list where the category "friend" and the category "acquaintance" merge, they might as well just go ahead and invite everybody they knew. So now we have a big wedding—a juggernaut, in fact. Because if you have all those people, you have to have a reception—you can't just say this is really a small wedding, so everybody go out somewhere for coffee. And, of course, if you are going to have all those people and a reception, then you can't just have a dinky little wedding and be embarrassed in front of all those people. No sir. The long white dress, rented tuxedos, flowers, attendants, photographers, rings—the whole kit and kaboodle. All because they thought having just a few more people would be a nice idea. Guess what comes next? Right.

Plan D: They can't do the whole hoo-ha and not invite the families. Mine field, here we come.

(*I note in passing that weddings always tend to get a little out of hand. I've never seen one get smaller or stay in budget. One thing always leads to another. It's kind of like marriage itself. Or life. And why not? When it comes to joy and celebration, let it be expansive, always.*)

Anyhow. They stepped on a mine. The Big One. Called their mothers and invited them to the wedding. The couple called from my house, and the phone hasn't worked right since. Probably fried the wires all the way back to Detroit and Brooklyn. The mothers were united in their response. "YOU'RE MARRYING A WHAT? A WHAT!" followed by silence and a lot of sobbing. Then the daddies got on the line and the sum of their remarks was, "COME HOME NOW, THIS MINUTE, NOW."

For a month the mail and phone calls flowed like a waterfall. Uncles and aunts and cousins got in the fray. The rabbi wrote a thirty-page letter. The priests and nun prayed. The families were NOT COMING, EVER, to such a wedding. The families threatened blackmail, hellfire, and heartbreak. Bribes were offered. No matter; nothing could dissuade the couple. Not even being disinherited, which was the ultimate threat thrown at them by both families.

Not that the bride and groom were unmoved.

They spent a lot of time in the Reverend Mr. Fulghum's office—the bride bawled, the groom swore.
But the marriage was meant to be, come hell or high
water, both of which seemed well on their way. But
the couple had an invisible shield: Love. And a secret
weapon: a sense of humor—light hearts. They
laughed as often as they cried.

Too, they came from tough, resilient folks who
had made it the hard way and had always told their
kids not to back off when they believed in something.
The kids were doing exactly what their parents had
taught them to do. They believed in each other. And
that was that.

The tiebreaker in this standoff was a grandma. The
grandmother of the groom. By God, if her only
grandson was getting married, no matter to a YOU-
KNOW-WHAT, then she was going to be there. For
the sake of the unborn grandchildren who would
need her. Besides, she hadn't approved of her
daughter-in-law, either, but that had worked out just
fine, thank you. Granny was serious—she went and
bought a ticket—SHE was coming to the wedding.
Period.

Thus the dominoes fell. If Grandmother was coming, then she would need support—she couldn't go
alone, of course—and pretty soon all the Irish Catholics from Detroit were coming. They'd show those
Jewish yahoos from Brooklyn what real FAMILY

LOYALTY was all about. And they'd bring Uncle
Dickie, the priest, to keep things as godly as possible.

Well. You know what happened next. Thirty-five
Brooklyn Jews, including Grandfather Rabbi, had
plane tickets.

The wedding began to shape up like a grudge
match between Notre Dame and Jerusalem Tech. In
physics they call this "achieving a critical mass."

Sure enough, they all came. And then it really got
complicated. The grandfather rabbi begged to at least
be allowed to say a traditional blessing in Hebrew at
the end of the service. When the Irish Catholics got
wind of this, nothing would do but that the grandmother, who had once performed in light opera,
should sing Schubert's "Ave Maria" before the blessing, as a kind of prophylactic to the Hebrew. One
side wanted a little incense used, and the other wanted
to have some wine in the ceremony and then break
the goblet. The bride and groom could do little but
nod their heads and smile and say "Whatever" to
whatever was proposed.

Come the great day, Saturday evening—after sun-
down, to please the you-know-whats—the families
marched into the church and sat down—no, "dug in"
would be the more accurate phrase, on either side of
the aisle. For a time I would have given 6-to-5 odds in

favor of a free-for-all following the ceremony instead of a reception.

Ah, but I keep forgetting about Love. The Irish Catholics from Detroit loved the groom; no less than the Polish Jews from Brooklyn loved the bride. And for very good reasons—they were remarkable young people, worthy of pride and respect, even if they didn't have a brain in their heads when it came to choosing a mate. And even the most bitter, jaundiced critic of the match had a hard time ignoring how tall and handsome the groom was or how enchanting was the bride. And you'd have to be really blind to miss what happened during the ceremony—when the couple said their vows, it was clear they meant every word. And when the bride began to weep and her groom took her in his arms and wept, too—well, the whole church was awash in tears. I've seen wet weddings before, but this turned into a communal bath. The whole thing ground to a halt while everybody had a good cry. The minister included. Even Uncle Dickie the priest, lurking out in the vestibule lest he get contaminated by the proceedings, was seen dabbing his eyes and blowing his nose.

What was happening was simple, really. Joy had jumped us all from behind about the time the bride said, "Yes, oh yes, YES!" when the minister asked if she took this man, etc. Something very old and fine and new and good was plainly happening. Only a head or heart of stone would have missed it. Joy. Unspeakable affirmation of something right. So we wept on, for lack of words.

It was then that the grandmother of the groom— the grand matriarch of the Irish Catholics, seventy-eight years old—rose to sing "Ave Maria." She did not come all this way to let her grandson down. She stood by the piano, took a deep breath, closed her eyes, and delivered the goods. Never have I heard the song offered with more feeling, more passion and fervor. She was magnificent. Not the scratchy, over-dramatic sounds you might expect from an aging third-rate opera singer. No. This was the voice of a grandmother distilling her life into the music for a once-in-a-lifetime occasion to honor what she loved and believed in. When the last lovely note faded and silence held us firm, Grandmother opened her eyes, smiled at her grandson, and said, "There, now."

And the Brooklyn Jews gave her a spontaneous standing ovation. They might not have known what was proper to do in a church, but they knew music and they knew that Grandma had given it all she had—and they knew great love when they saw it. She was their kind of guy. And a standing O was called for. Yea, Grandma!

Grandfather Rabbi was not about to be outdone. He walked slowly to stand close by the bride and groom. He reached out and took their hands in his. And then, speaking for Abraham, Isaac, Jacob, and all the Jews of Brooklyn, he laid a blessing on the couple that ought to last them the rest of their lives. I mean they were BLESSED, and you didn't have to understand Hebrew to know it.

So, of course, as you would hope, the Irish Catholics gave Grandfather Rabbi a standing ovation he will never forget. Yea, Grandpa!

That's when the minister sighed a deep sigh of relief, knowing that Joy had won the day, and the possibility of a happy ending to this affair was real. A happy ending. More than anything else in this life, we hope for some happy endings. And we were about to have one.

What the families had not understood until the end of the wedding was that they had many of the same values and traditions, despite their arguments over metaphors for ultimate things. They believed in family, faith, love, the same God, and the capacity to celebrate those things.

The bride and groom rushed off down the aisle to the reception hall, where a polka band was waiting. The newlyweds danced and everyone applauded. Grandfather Rabbi asked Grandmother Opera Singer to dance, and the crowd roared and then joined them and the party was on. Never have I been to such a reception—never was there such dancing and eating and laughing and singing—long, long into the night. Magnificent!

Three days later, when my head cleared, I wondered how it had happened. And decided that the skeptical minister had been wrong and the bride and groom right. Love was more powerful than prejudice—Love won out. I don't know that I am totally convinced, but in this case it's what the evidence points at. The final score was Love—21, Evil Spirits—zip. When in doubt, trust those you love—all of them.

(*Epilogue. A year later, close to the first anniversary of this amazing occasion, I received a postcard mailed from a cruise ship in the Caribbean. From the bride and groom, I thought. No. From the parents of the bride and the groom, who have become great friends.*)

WEDDINGS ARE USUALLY THOUGHT OF AS FAIRY-TALE times when Real Life is momentarily suspended. "And they lived happily ever after" seems possible, if only for a day. When my children were small and their daddy tried to end bedtime stories with the happy ending, one of them would always ask, "And THEN what happened?" How could I tell them that Cinderella discovered she was married to a guy with a foot fetish and that glass slippers hurt like hell? How could I tell them that the frog who was kissed by the princess might have turned into a prince, but still had the personality of a frog and ate flies for breakfast instead of cereal? What I know about real life suggests those are not unreasonable answers to the and-then-what-happened question.

I tell couples, in mock seriousness, that the warranty on the wedding license is only good for twenty-four hours. The odds on a marriage lasting are 50–50 now, which means that a minister is often asked to perform a wedding wherein one or both parties have been previously married. They did not live happily ever after the first time around. But they know something now—about themselves, about real life, and about marriage. And their weddings reflect their wisdom.

For one thing, they know, as I know, that the real wedding and the real vows don't happen on the day of the formal social occasion.

There comes a time, usually some days after the proposal and acceptance, after the announcement and setting of the date and all the rest, when there is a conversation between two people in love, when they are in earnest about what they've agreed to do. The conversation happens over several days—even weeks. Partly in a car driving somewhere, partly at a kitchen table after supper, partly on the living-room floor, or maybe on the way home after a movie. It's a conversation about promises, homes, family, children, possessions, jobs, dreams, rights, concessions, money, personal space, and all the problems that might arise from all those things. And what is promised at that time, in a disorganized, higgledy-piggledy way, is the making of a covenant. A covenant—an invisible bond of commitment. Just two people working out what they want, what they believe, what they hope for each other. With their eyes, they ask each other if they really mean it, and they do. Then they seal it with a whole lot more kissing and hugging than you'll see in public. And that's it. The wedding is done. All that's left to do is the public celebration, however they choose to do it.

I know this sounds like heresy—that the Church Fathers might not agree. But if you are married, you know it's true. That's why I always tell couples to pay more attention to what's going on in that talking time before the Big Day. They wouldn't want to miss their own wedding.

When couples come to me for a second marriage, they have always spent most of their time and energy on that talking time and are a lot less concerned about the Big Day than they were the first time. They know that companionship in the kitchen around suppertime is vastly more important than the color of the brides-maids' dresses. They know that good company and friendship count for more than good looks. And they know that marrying a frog is fine if you really like the frog a whole lot and don't expect princely transfor-mations. (*It's also what you know if the first marriage worked and you are about five years into it and plan to stay.*) It's not as romantic the second time, but it's not without love. The love tends to be richer, deeper, wiser this time.

These last several paragraphs are background to a fine story. Two brothers married at about the same

age—early twenties—over in the Dakotas somewhere. One brother was handsome, the catch of the
town. The other was a real toad: short and squatty,
and he loved to sing in a toady voice. The handsome
brother married a beautiful woman, and the toad
married a frog. The couples lived close by one
another and raised families together. Neither couple
was really happy—they had workable marriages, but
not satisfactory ones. But an outsider to the relation-
ships would never know the truth. The children grew
up and made marriages of their own. The handsome
brother died of a sudden heart attack at age fifty, and
the wife of the toad was killed in an automobile
accident.

I learned all this history when the surviving brother
and the surviving wife came to Seattle to consult with
me. They had looked upon one another with abiding
but secret love for years. After the two deaths, the
toad brother had started coming over to his sister-
in-law's house to keep a little company, and they
would have supper together and would do the dishes
together in the kitchen, singing old hymns while they
worked. They sometimes worked in her garden
together, pulling weeds, talking for hours about life
in general.

Neither one would say anything about feelings—in
a small town there was something not quite right

about a couple of widowed in-laws being in love or doing anything about it. But one night he was drying plates and started singing "I Love You Truly." She chimed in and he looked her in the eye and she looked back and they knew.

So. They began that long conversation that is the real wedding. Their first concern was, "What will our children think?" Their combined kids would be both sons and daughters and nieces and nephews; cousins and half-brothers and half-sisters. And some of the children were married and not doing too well at it. A family shake-up might tip some boats already tossing around in heavy seas.

But their love was long and wise, their lives short and lonely, and they had already married in the deepest sense—they had made the covenant of companionship.

They decided to elope. Imagine. To run away and get married. Through friends of friends they found me in Seattle and asked for confidential help in getting married.

What they didn't know was that their kids knew everything all along. About the marriages that were unhappy, about the silent endurance, about the love that had bloomed and the wedding that was happening there in the kitchen. Their kids had known and watched and learned a great deal about love and marriage in the process. Their kids had moved from dismay at what might happen to fervent hope that it would happen.

I knew the kids knew because I got a call from a daughter the same evening I talked with her mom and uncle. She had tracked them down and wanted to know if I was going to marry them and when, because the whole family was coming to the wedding somehow.

This was the fairy-tale part of the wedding. The blessing placed on it by the children of the bride and groom who came in a ten-car caravan all the way from Fargo, North Dakota. When the bride and groom walked through the front door of my house that Sunday afternoon for what they thought was going to be a simple, quiet ceremony, their children and grandchildren were hiding in my kitchen and back hall. As the bride and groom stood before me, their families came quietly into the room, faces wreathed in smiles, tears streaming down their faces. Such a moment. Such a moment.

A grandchild pulled the plug out of the emotional dam by shrieking "SURPRISE, SURPRISE!" and the whole gathering turned into a joyful hugging-and-kissing contest.

When some order and quiet were restored, the bride and groom and their children and grandchildren turned to me for the ceremony. And I said that what had just happened was about as fine a ceremony as I could think of, and I pronounced them husband and wife and aunt and uncle. Which started the hugging and kissing and yelling all over again. Acts, not words, are the ties that bind.

For years now I have told this story to couples who are making a second marriage. The point of the story is not that it had a happy ending. The point is that getting married for lust or money or social status or even love is usually trouble. The point is that marriage is a maze into which we wander—a maze that is best got through with a great companion—like a toad that sings while he washes dishes, for example. Or a beautiful woman who makes a toad feel like a prince when she holds his hand. That's the kind of fairy tale you can believe in.

"LIMMINAID 5 SINTS." Large, red-lettered ambitious sign of summer. Just down the block is the classic setup. Couple of sunburned kids, card table, kitchen chair, pitcher, paper cups, and the sign taped to a picket fence. It was their grandmother's idea at first. Get the kids out from underfoot and sitting in one place for a while. *(You can see her face in the kitchen window, keeping tabs on them.)*

The kids balked at first—they smelled a rat. But when they found out there was money to be made, basic capitalistic greed took over, and they've been out there every day for a week now. They've even started watering down their product to increase profits.

I know. Because for five days now I have been their best customer. I also know because I was in the lemonade racket myself as a child.

So I keep them in business by taking unnecessary trips around the block to pass by their stand. It's a good deal for them. And me. For five cents, I get a cup of lemon-flavored water and a dash of nostalgia, and they improve their cash position. I am a favored customer. They gave me the last dregs of a pitcher at the end of the working day for free. Now I know where the sugar was all this time.

And they are better businessmen than I was at their age. It is the job of the youngest kid to follow customers and take back the cup before it is thrown away. I thought they were preventing littering. But it turns out they were reusing the cups. "Isn't that a bit unsanitary?" "Why? You got some disease?" What could I say?

I offered to provide them with cookies to expand their range of merchandise. I would sell them the cookies for a nickel and they could sell them for a dime. They are at the age when if an adult offers to do you a favor, you look upon it with great suspicion. But the next day there were cookies on the card table. Fifteen cents a cookie, too. "Grandmother made them. She GAVE them to us." *(Grandmother smiles and waves at me from the kitchen window.)* I am up against economic forces I cannot defeat, and brains wiser than mine. My job is to be the customer. No middlemen need apply.

This is not the first time I have been the pigeon in a game run by two generations of blood kin.

On a lumpy road in the highlands of the island of Corsica one summer, an urchin flagged down my car, waving and pointing at something in a basket. I stopped. Behind him was an elderly man sitting at a table. Tall green bottles on the table.

The kid flashes me a ten-dollar gap-toothed grin.

"Mister, you speak English?"

I nod. And the mini-merchant comes close and speaks in conspiratorial tones: "My poor old grandfather is selling almonds and wine. The almonds are from his trees, and he makes the wine himself. The almonds are okay, but the wine is very terrible. But it is cheap. Please buy some and make my poor grandfather happy, okay?"

Another lemonade dealer. And the League of Lemonade Dealers has to stick together, right? So. For about a dollar I got a small sack of almonds and two bottles of wine. The kid smiles and the old man smiles and I smile. The conspiracy holds.

And the kid was right. No false advertising here. The almonds were pretty tasty. The wine, ghastly.

Several miles later on is another kid and another old man and the same story. Coincidence. And for another buck I have another sack of almonds and two more bottles of premier rotgut.

But several more miles and there was another kid and another old man, and a few more miles down the road still another. In twenty miles I counted eleven sets of friendly holdup artists.

I found out that night in the village that the old men hire the young boys, who have learned English in school, to flag down the tourists and tell the story, and it always works. I also learned that the old men do not understand the intricacies of the foreign exchange, but the little boys do. What the urchins collect from the tourists and what they give to the old men is not the same.

I suspect that the old men are not that confused about what is going on, either, but considering that they are selling watered vinegar as wine, they can't complain about being stung a little by the larceny of the younger generation.

Everybody is in on the scam.

Even me. I gave two bottles of the wine to a taxi driver as a tip. He overcharged me when he took me from my hotel to the ferry, but I didn't speak enough French to argue with him. He was pleased to get the wine, though. Maybe when he finds out about the wine, he will give it to the old man by the road with the little boy and it will go round again.

A year later, on a back street in the city of Heraklion on the island of Crete. Two kids, a rickety table, some glasses, a pitcher, a sign—the usual equipment.

"Hey, mister, you speak English?"

Here we go again.

"Sure, what are you selling?"

"Super Cola—my grandfather made it."

As I recall, Super Cola is just a Greek soft drink.

"How much?"

"One American dollar."

"A dollar for a bottle of Super Cola? That's crazy."

"Wait till you taste it."

You just can't let a fellow limminaid dealer down, so I paid my dollar, picked up a bottle, and took a big drink.

In the bottle is raki—the local version of white lightning—raw hooch. Some people have been known to levitate after drinking it, I am told. Others have not been able to describe the experience. Because they can't talk anymore.

I walked away in a warm glow, my lips a little numb, but feeling pretty loose and fine. Now THAT'S what I call LEMONADE!

If you are ever in my neighborhood in the summertime, and you see a middle-aged man in a floppy hat, sitting by a card table under a sign that says EXTRA SPECIAL LEMONADE, $1, stop by and have a drink in the name of the international brotherhood of limminaid sellers.

1969. A SIGN: ANYWHERE BUT HERE. Held by three waifish flower children standing at a freeway entrance looking for a ride on the great river of adventure. Common sign of that time—saw it more than once, and felt it in people many times. Wanderlust mixed with discontent.

Recently saw another sign by the freeway entrance. SOMEWHERE ELSE AND BACK. Liked the spirit of the sign, so I pulled over and the travelers piled gratefully into my truck. Young university students, male and female—one of each. Tired of "here"—taking a semester off to go see it all, wherever IT is.

"But your sign says 'and back.' "

"Well, this is home, you know, and we like it here. We just want to be somewhere else for a while. You ever feel that way?"

"About once a week, actually."

When people are polled on what they would do if

they won the lottery, first they'd pay their bills and then they would travel—go see the world, go somewhere else and back. Nomads we are, at heart. And it always amuses me when anthropologists find the ruins of civilizations that seem to have been suddenly abandoned. What caused this? Where did they go? What was the problem? No problem, really, they just woke up one morning in a collective mood to be somewhere else. They went. And just didn't quite make it back.

Count up the number of places you have lived so far in your life. Thirty-seven places in fifty-one years—that's my record—and my wife and I are talking where-to-and-what-next again. Restlessness is our way, and we scratch the itch when we can. Having traveled "somewhere else and back" quite a few times now, here are two elemental truths I know:

First: The grass is not, in fact, always greener on the other side of the fence. No, not at all. Fences have nothing to do with it. The grass is greenest where it is watered. When crossing over fences, carry water with you and tend the grass wherever you may be.

Second: The River-Runner's Maxim, taught to me when I was learning white-water canoeing from friend Baz, a maximum pro: "Sitting still is essential to the journey." When heading off downriver, pull over to the bank from time to time and sit quietly and look at the river and think about where you've been and where you're going and why and how.

So. Come sit by me on the bank and I will tell you where the grass is green and what I know about the river. . . .

"GREEK PHILOSOPHY LIVES!" Scrawled in English on a doorway in the Plaka, the ancient marketplace tucked beneath the great stone walls of the Acropolis. The heart of Athens. It's true. They are still at it, the Greeks. Philosophy is not entombed forever in 4 B.C. or buried in college textbooks to burden sophomores. It lives. As surely as the Greeks themselves live.

The winning brand is pragmatism. From *pragma*—"deed." This is the philosophical doctrine that the test of the truth of propositions is their practical result. Never mind what you say or think. What you do and how it works out—that's what counts. You can read all about pragmatism in the philosophy books. Or you can just watch the Greeks go about their business. The stories that follow come from watching.

At the airport in Chania, on the west end of the island of Crete, an Olympia Airlines 727 disgorges a hundred yelling passengers into the crowded terminal. Bedlam. Fists and voices raised, women weeping, children wailing. Two passengers leap over a counter to take a punch at the attendant. Police arrive, whistles shrieking, billy clubs in hand.

Explanation: The passengers were all destined for Heraklion, at the other end of the island. Where, indeed, their luggage has gone by another plane. For reasons unknown, their plane has landed at the wrong city and left the passengers to a hard ride by bus 150 miles to their destination. The passengers want blood. The passengers declare they will commandeer a plane. What the passengers think of those responsible cannot be printed here, but it's pretty harsh and involves the parenthood and birth of those who run Olympia Airlines and where they may spend eternity.

One passenger, a stout, well-dressed German tourist who has been pacing in small circles on the edge of the chaos, suddenly begins to shout alternately in German and English: "WHY AM I HERE? WHERE AM I GOING? WHAT MUST I DO? WHAT WILL BECOME OF ME? GOTT IM HIMMEL, HELP ME!"

His desperate cry is so forceful that the crowd quiets and turns to look at him with concern, as they would consider a mad dog in their midst.

The airline station manager replies in English across the crowd: "Sir! Sir! These are very old questions. We Greeks have been working on them for two thousand years and they are not easy to answer—not then, not now. In the meantime we will do our best for you. The gods will not be of much help, but Olympia Airlines will see that you get to Heraklion. Please. Get on the bus."

The crowd applauds. The passengers file out into the bus, which roars off toward Heraklion. Leaving the German tourist limp, still muttering questions and demanding reasonable answers.

That afternoon, in a sidewalk café on the seafront esplanade of Chania, I overheard two young Americans arguing over whether human beings were basically bad or basically good. Law students they were. First year. One pointed to his glass of wine and sagely insisted that this question was like whether his wineglass was half full or half empty—a matter of words and opinion. His companion disagreed. "Not so, not so—the precise amount of wine in a glass can be determined with scientific tools, and a definition of full and empty can be agreed upon. That old cliché can be laid to rest!"

He motioned for the waiter and asked for two empty glasses and something to measure with. Science would provide an answer here, just as sound thinking would resolve the larger issue of human nature.

The waiter, an old Greek man of solemn years,

asked the purpose of the request, and all was explained to him. The waiter looked at the two young men. Then at the glass of wine to be tested for truth. He smiled. Picked up the glass of wine and held it to his nose to smell the aroma. Lifted it in a wordless toast to each of the young travelers and drank it down with relish. He smiled. And walked away.

Pragmatism. A time to shout and a time to get on the bus. A time to debate and a time to drink the wine.

FAR TO THE SOUTH AND WEST OF ATHENS, on the rocky coast of the Peloponnesian peninsula, is the village of Stupa/Lefktron. Though not on a standard travel map, it is important as the place where Nikos Kazantzakis wrote his novel *Zorba,* the greatest modern expression of Greek pragmatism.

Stupa/Lefktron has had a divided name since the Turkish occupation (before 1883), and is divided today into about thirty-five different political parties—which means there are thirty-five men in the village who can vote. The village is united on two fronts, however.

First is a burning desire to make as much money out of the tourists as possible in July and August. The other common bond is religion. Greek Orthodox.

It would be easy, one might think, for economics and religion to come into conflict during tourist season, when who has time to spend Sunday morning in church when everybody is working the cafés and crafts shops and restaurants to get the last drachma out of the tour-bus travelers?

No problem.

In the early morning quiet, Father Michaelis has set up a tape deck and speakers in the church courtyard on the hill above the village. And he is broadcasting the service to the village as he sits in his chair taking coffee brought up to him from one of the cafés.

The mass is three hours long and is always the same and everybody knows it by heart, so it is enough that they hear it and follow it in their hearts as they go about their business. From nine until noon, the village is the church. "Wherever they are, God is also there," Father Michaelis explained to me, "and whatever they are doing, God is with them. It is no problem. To them, to me, or to God."

"And what if the bishop in Athens finds out about this?"

"Who is going to tell him? And if someone should, who knows? The idea may catch on. It is true that the village should be in church. And so it shall be when September comes. But for now, it is enough that the church is everywhere in the village. Is it not the same, after all?"

SPEAKING OF RELIGION, HAVE YOU EVER HAD GREEK coffee? Only a few non-Greeks have had more than a couple of cups at one time and lived to talk about it. But if you are a serious coffee drinker, and you don't mind being wide awake for forty-eight hours, and your health insurance is paid up, and you don't mind your tongue and teeth tasting like the bottom of a bird cage, and you are used to massive heartburn, then you will just love Greek coffee.

My first cup was at the fall bazaar at St. Demetrios Greek Orthodox Church in Seattle. Compliments of Constanzia Gregocopoulos, somebody's eighty-four-year-old grandmother, visiting from Athens. When she tasted the coffee the church was serving, she raised a ruckus. Said that proper Greek coffee must be served or else. So there she was that afternoon, dressed all in black, surrounded by brass pots and hot plates and roasted coffee beans—also black. Like a sorceress, she bent over her work, muttering to her interpreter.

"I'd like a cup of coffee now," say I.

"Πρέπει νά περιμένεις," says Mrs. Gregocopoulos. (*She is almost deaf and bellows a bit at me and her assistant.*)

"She says you must wait."

"Ask her why."

"Οί 'Αμερικανοί όλο θέλουν άμέσος, άλλά δέν είναι όλο άμέσος καλά."

"She says Americans always want everything NOW and getting everything now is not always good."

" Ὁ Θεός ἔκανε ἑπτά μέρες γιά νά κάνη τόν κόσμο καί τόν ἔκανε ὀρέα διόση δέν διάστικε."

"She says God took seven days to make the world and it was good because He took his time and wasn't in a hurry."

"Ἐγώ, Κωνστάνζια Γρεγοκόπουλος, Θέλω ἀκριβός ἑπτά λεπτά γιά τόν καφέ εἶς τό ὄνομα τόν Θεόυ."

"She says that she, Constanzia Gregocopoulos, takes exactly seven minutes to make coffee, in the spirit of God."

"Θά περιμένεις καί Θά τό φτιάσο καί Θά τό πινίς καί Θά σού αρέσει."

"She says you will wait and she will make and you will drink and you will like!"

"Yes, ma'am," says I.

And I did and she did and I did and I really did.

"IS GOOD, YES?" she bellows in my ear.

"Yes, ma'am," says I.

"Θά μάθεις νά περιμένεις καί ὁ Θεός Θά σέ εὐλογίση ποιό συχνά καί Θά ζίσης νά γεράσης χαρούμενος."

"She says to learn to wait and God will bless you more often and you will live to be old and happy."

The old lady laughed a toothless laugh and pinched

my cheek in the affectionate way shown to fools who still may find wisdom.

"ARE THERE ANY QUESTIONS?" An offer that comes at the end of college lectures and long meetings. Said when an audience is not only overdosed with information, but when there is no time left anyhow. At times like that you sure do have questions. Like, "Can we leave now?" and "What the hell was this meeting for?" and "Where can I get a drink?"

The gesture is supposed to indicate openness on the part of the speaker, I suppose, but if in fact you do ask a question, both the speaker and the audience will give you drop-dead looks. And some fool—some earnest idiot—always asks. And the speaker always answers. By repeating most of what he has already said.

But if there is a little time left and there is a little silence in response to the invitation, I usually ask the most important question of all: "What is the Meaning of Life?"

You never know, somebody may have the answer, and I'd really hate to miss it because I was too socially inhibited to ask. But when I ask, it's usually taken as a kind of absurdist move—people laugh and nod and gather up their stuff and the meeting is dismissed on that ridiculous note.

Once, and only once, I asked that question and got a serious answer. One that is with me still.

First, I must tell you where this happened, because the place has a power of its own. In Greece again.

Near the village of Gonia on a rocky bay of the island of Crete, sits a Greek Orthodox monastery. Alongside it, on land donated by the monastery, is an institute dedicated to human understanding and peace, and especially to rapprochement between Germans and Cretans. An improbable task, given the bitter residue of wartime.

This site is important, because it overlooks the small airstrip at Maleme where Nazi paratroopers invaded Crete and were attacked by peasants wielding kitchen knives and hay scythes. The retribution was terrible. The populations of whole villages were lined up and shot for assaulting Hitler's finest troops. High above the institute is a cemetery with a single cross marking the mass grave of Cretan partisans. And across the bay on yet another hill is the regimented burial ground of the Nazi paratroopers. The memorials are so placed that all might see and never forget. Hate was the only weapon the Cretans had at the end, and it was a weapon many vowed never to give up. Never ever.

Against this heavy curtain of history, in this place

where the stone of hatred is hard and thick, the existence of an institute devoted to healing the wounds of war is a fragile paradox. How has it come to be here? The answer is a man. Alexander Papaderos.

A doctor of philosophy, teacher, politician, resident of Athens but a son of this soil. At war's end he came to believe that the Germans and the Cretans had much to give one another—much to learn from one another. That they had an example to set. For if they could forgive each other and construct a creative relationship, then any people could.

To make a lovely story short, Papaderos succeeded. The institute became a reality—a conference ground on the site of horror—and it was in fact a source of productive interaction between the two countries. Books have been written on the dreams that were realized by what people gave to people in this place.

By the time I came to the institute for a summer session, Alexander Papaderos had become a living legend. One look at him and you saw his strength and intensity—energy, physical power, courage, intelligence, passion, and vivacity radiated from his person. And to speak to him, to shake his hand, to be in a room with him when he spoke, was to experience his extraordinary electric humanity. Few men live up to their reputations when you get close. Alexander Papaderos was an exception.

At the last session on the last morning of a two-week seminar on Greek culture, led by intellectuals and experts in their fields who were recruited by Papaderos from across Greece, Papaderos rose from his chair at the back of the room and walked to the front, where he stood in the bright Greek sunlight of an open window and looked out. We followed his gaze across the bay to the iron cross marking the German cemetery.

He turned. And made the ritual gesture: "Are there any questions?"

Quiet quilted the room. These two weeks had generated enough questions for a lifetime, but for now there was only silence.

"No questions?" Papaderos swept the room with his eyes.

So. I asked.

"Dr. Papaderos, what is the meaning of life?"

The usual laughter followed, and people stirred to go.

Papaderos held up his hand and stilled the room and looked at me for a long time, asking with his eyes if I was serious and seeing from my eyes that I was.

"I will answer your question."

Taking his wallet out of his hip pocket, he fished into a leather billfold and brought out a very small round mirror, about the size of a quarter.

And what he said went like this:

"When I was a small child, during the war, we were very poor and we lived in a remote village. One day, on the road, I found the broken pieces of a mirror. A German motorcycle had been wrecked in that place.

"I tried to find all the pieces and put them together, but it was not possible, so I kept only the largest piece. This one. And by scratching it on a stone I made it round. I began to play with it as a toy and became fascinated by the fact that I could reflect light into dark places where the sun would never shine—in deep holes and crevices and dark closets. It became a game for me to get light into the most inaccessible places I could find.

"I kept the little mirror, and as I went about my growing up, I would take it out in idle moments and continue the challenge of the game. As I became a man, I grew to understand that this was not just a child's game but a metaphor for what I might do with my life. I came to understand that I am not the light or the source of light. But light—truth, understanding, knowledge—is there, and it will only shine in many dark places if I reflect it.

"I am a fragment of a mirror whose whole design and shape I do not know. Nevertheless, with what I have I can reflect light into the dark places of this world—into the black places in the hearts of men—and change some things in some people. Perhaps others may see and do likewise. This is what I am about. This is the meaning of my life."

And then he took his small mirror and, holding it carefully, caught the bright rays of daylight streaming through the window and reflected them onto my face and onto my hands folded on the desk.

Much of what I experienced in the way of information about Greek culture and history that summer is gone from memory. But in the wallet of my mind I carry a small round mirror still.

Are there any questions?

O NCE ON A MIDSUMMER'S EVE, in the farming village of Puyricard, near Aix-en-Provence in the south of France, my wife and I were taken to a celebration of the Feast of Saint John. (Which Saint John I do not know. There are many. If he provided a reason to celebrate with music and dance, then good on him, whoever he was.)

When the first star could be seen in the night sky, the villagers lit a bonfire in the dirty playfield of the school, and a folk band began to play—guitar, bass drum, shepherd's flute and concertina. Music that was close at hand and long ago at the same time. In a universal two-step, couples danced, encircling the great fire—their only light. Lovely. A scene from a novel, a film, a hopeful imagination.

At the first intermission, the couples did not leave for refreshment, but stood staring into the bonfire. Suddenly an athletic young man and woman, holding each other tightly by the hand, ran and leaped high in the air through the fierce flames, landing safely just beyond the edge of the coals. As the crowd applauded, the two embraced and walked away, wearing expressions of fearful joy, having tempted the fates and emerged unscathed to dance once more. Make no mistake about it, what they had done was quite dangerous.

And it was this leaping through the fire that was at the heart of the Feast of Saint John.

It worked this way: If you were lovers, married or not, or if you were just friends, even, and you wanted to seal your covenant, you made a wish together that you would never part, and then you rushed the fire and jumped over while holding hands. It was said that the hotter the fire and the higher the flames, the longer and closer would be the companionship. But it was also said that if you misjudged the fire and got singed or came down in the coals on the other side or lost your grip on one another while jumping, then evil would come to you and your bond. Not to be taken lightly, this.

So the young of heart and fleet of foot jumped early on; as the evening grew darker and the fire burned lower, the more cautious made their moves. Some did not clear the fire; some jumped too soon and some too late and some ran to the fire only to stop short, and some broke their grip, with one partner jumping while the other held back at the last moment.

Though there was much laughter and cheering and teasing, it was also very clear that this was ancient and serious business. Not just another party. Once a year, late in the night of high summer, with music and dance to lift the spirit, you took your love by the hand and tempted the fire of destiny.

At evening's end, when only glowing coals remained, there was played a traditional tune signaling a last dance. As the final note of the shepherd's flute faded, the villagers encircled the soft glow of the embers and fell silent. The village couple married longest caught hands, and gracefully, solemnly, stepped together over what once was fire. At that signal of benediction, the villagers embraced and walked off into the starry, starry night toward home, and all the fires of love ever after. . . .

AMERICANS, IT IS OBSERVED, PREFER DEFINITE answers. Let your yea-yea be your yea-yea, and your nay-nay be your nay-nay. Yes or no. No grays please.

In Indonesia, there is a word in common use that nicely wires around the need for black and white. *Belum* is the word and it means "not quite yet." A lovely word implying continuing possibility. "Do you speak English?" *"Belum."* Not quite yet. "Do you have any children?" *"Belum."* "Do you know the meaning of life?" *"Belum."* It is considered both impolite and cynical to say "No" outright. This leads to some funny moments. "Is the taxi on fire?" *"Belum."* Not quite yet.

It's an attitude kin to that behind the old vaudeville joke: "Do you play the violin?" "I don't know, I never tried."

Perhaps. Maybe. Possibly. Not yes or no, but

within the realm of what might be. Soft edges are
welcome in this great bus ride of human adventure.

Is this the best of all possible worlds? *Belum*.

Is the world coming to an end? *Belum*.

Will we live happily ever after? *Belum*.

Can we do without the weapons of war?

I don't know, we never tried.

Is it hopeless to think we might?

Belum. Not yet.

THE SPIRE OF THE GREAT CATHEDRAL IN ULM, GER-
many, is the tallest steeple in the world—529 feet.
Seven hundred thirty-eight stone steps take you to the
very top. I counted them. And if you can still breathe
and focus your eyes when you get there, you can
make out two prominent landmarks: the foothills of
the Bavarian Alps south of town, and the high bluffs
overlooking the Danube River to the east.

In the late sixteenth century, Hans Ludwig Babblinger lived here. A maker of artificial limbs, a
craftsman with special skills and some local fame for
those skills. Since amputation was a common cure for
ills and wounds, he was a busy man. As his hands
worked, his mind was often elsewhere. For Babblinger was one of those who imagined he could fly.

In due course, he used his skills and dreams and the
materials in his shop to craft wings. And as fortune
would have it, he chose to try his wings in the

foothills of the Bavarian Alps, where upcurrents abounded. One day, one wonderful day, in the presence of reliable witnesses, Hans jumped off a high hill and soared safely down. Sensational! Babblinger could FLY!

Shift of time and scene. It is the spring of 1594. King Ludwig and his court are coming to Ulm for a visit, and the city leaders want to impress him. "Get Hans Ludwig Babblinger to fly for the king!" Of course.

Unfortunately, because it suited the convenience of the king and the townspeople, Babblinger chose the nearby bluffs of the Danube for his demonstration. The winds there are downcurrents.

The great day arrived—musicians, the king and his court, the town fathers, thousands of ordinary folk, all gathered at the river. Babblinger stood on a high platform on the bluffs, waved, crouched, and threw himself into the air.

And went down into the river like a cannonball. Not good.

The next Sunday, from the pulpit of the great cathedral, the Bishop of Ulm called Babblinger by name during the sermon and shamed him for the sin of pride.

"MAN WAS NOT MEANT TO FLY!" thundered the prelate.

Cringing under the accusing wrath of the bishop,

Babblinger walked out of the church to his house, never to appear in public again. Not long after, he died. With his wings and dreams and heart broken.

Recently I was a passenger in a glider surfing on a thermal wave at five thousand feet. Babblinger and the Bishop of Ulm came to mind. Below me I could see a hot-air balloon, an ultralight aircraft, other gliders, and three parachutists swinging down from the sky. Above us, a 747 wheeled east toward Chicago, slanted up toward thirty-eight thousand feet.

How I wished I could call Hans Babblinger from his grave to a seat in the glider and say, "Look! Look and be not ashamed. Man *was* meant to fly."

Historically, the symbol of the pulpit has been the pointing, damning finger. Accusing men and women of sin, failure, wickedness, iniquities, and the pride of thinking for themselves. Preaching that on this earth there is no hope—in this life there is no glory.

I say the pulpit should stand for wings. Not angel wings or eagle wings or any other wings you've ever seen. Wings of the holy human spirit—wings that lift heart and mind to high places. Wings for all the Babblingers in our midst who will see them and leave inspired to try again and again to stretch human possibility.

Wings like that can't be seen, I guess. You have to

believe in them to see them in your imagination, and you have to take risks in dangerous places to see if they work.

Most of the people who go to the church at Ulm now are tourists. The few solemn folk who sit beneath the ancient pulpit during Sunday services are outnumbered by the hang-gliders flying in flocks off the foothills in the bright morning air in the great cathedral of the world.

Wherever you are, Hans Ludwig Babblinger, I thought you would like to know.

THE SUFIS ARE MYSTICS IN THE ISLAMIC TRADITION. Their leaders are famous for their teaching stories— short anecdotes that seem light and simple at first telling, but that contain a seed of great wisdom. The stories are never told as preachments. It is left to the hearer to do with them as he may choose and to take on whatever level of meaning suits him.

Thus it was explained by an Islamic scholar traveling with me on a bus in Switzerland. *(Retired teacher from Algeria, who was weary of hot, flat places and wanted to be in the mountains.)* These were his two favorite traveling tales from the Sufi masters.

A famous religious teacher—a saint, in fact—was passing through a small town. It was known that he carried with him the secret key to understanding the meaning of life. A certain pickpocket approached him, searched him with his talented fingers, found nothing, and turned away, empty-handed. All he had noticed were the pockets.

A famous teacher was invited by a prince to go lion hunting. When he returned, he was asked how the hunt had gone. "Marvelous!" And how many lions did they find? "None—that is why it was so marvelous."

SOMEWHERE OUT THERE IN THE WORLD IS A YOUNG woman who, if she reads the letter that follows, will sing out, "Hey, that's me—that's my story!" This letter is written out of gratitude—from me and all those who have heard her story from me. Out of one person's moment of comic despair has come perspective for all.

Dear Fellow Pilgrim:

There you were, Hong Kong airport, end of the summer of 1984, tensely occupying a chair next to mine. Everything about you said "Young American Traveler Going Home." You had by then exchanged jeans and T-shirt for sarong and sandals. Sensible short hair had given way to hair long and loose. The backpack beside you bore the scars and dirt of some hard traveling, and it bulged with mysterious souvenirs of seeing the world. Lucky kid, I thought.

When the tears began to drip from your chin, I imagined some lost love or the sorrow of giving up adventure for college classes. But when you began to sob, you drew me into your sadness. Guess you had been very alone and very brave for some time. A good cry was in order. And weep you did. All over me. A monsoon of grievous angst. My handkerchief and your handkerchief and most of a box of tissues and both your sleeves were needed to dry up the flood before you finally got it out.

Indeed, you were not quite ready to go home; you wanted to go further on. But you had run out of money and your friends had run out of money, and so here you were having spent two days waiting in the airport standby with little to eat and too much pride to beg. And your plane was about to go. And you had lost your ticket. You cried all over me again. You had been sitting in this one spot for three hours, sinking into the cold sea of despair like some torpedoed freighter. At moments you thought you would sit there until you died.

After we dried you off, I and a nice older couple from Chicago who were also swept away in the tide of your tears, offered to take you to lunch and to talk to the powers that be at the airlines about some remedy. You stood up to go with us, turned around to pick up your belongings. And SCREAMED. I thought you had been shot. But no . . . it was your *ticket*. You found your ticket. You had been *sitting* on it. For three hours.

Like a sinner saved from the very jaws of hell, you laughed and cried and hugged us all and were suddenly gone. Off to catch a plane for home and what next. Leaving most of the passenger lounge deliriously limp from being part of your drama.

I've told the story countless times. "She was sitting on her own ticket," I conclude, and the listeners always laugh in painful self-recognition.

Often when I have been sitting on my own ticket in some way—sitting on whatever it is I have that will get me up and on to what comes next—I think of you and grin at both of us and get moving.

So, thanks. You have become, in a special way, my travel agent. May you find all your tickets and arrive wherever it is you want to go, now and always.

*L*IKE MANY WESTERNERS IN THE LATE SIXTIES, I wanted to be somewhere else in my religious journey. Confusion reigned in the kingdom of my mind, and I yearned to construct a framework of understanding that seemed beyond my present cultural tools. I couldn't seem to get "there" from "here."

Zen and its idea of enlightenment appealed to me. That one might sit very still and empty one's mind and suddenly be hit by a mighty wave of comprehension beyond words—well, that would do. Hit me with the big news and let me walk away with a sense of "I get it!"

Took a leave of absence from my dailiness and went off to Japan to get Zenned properly. Got connected to a temple and a master. Shaved my head and face, put on the drab gray robe of the novitiate, and stood in line to get enlightened. Figured to become a pretty holy man in pretty short order, like in about six weeks, which was when my return ticket home expired. Right.

But of course it was not to be. Sitting still gave me hallucinations and cramps, but not enlightenment. The food gave me diarrhea. Sleeping on a board gave me a backache. And my fellow monks treated me like a Western fool, laughing at me behind my back. It was one of those times when you know enough to realize there's something everybody but you knows, but you don't know enough to know exactly what it is you don't know.

But I did know it was time to leave.

To my surprise, an invitation was extended for an interview with the master of the temple. Which was like a stockboy being asked to have lunch with the president of the company.

Since it was largely because of his reputation that I had chosen this particular temple, and since he rarely spent time with tourists like me, the master's invitation seemed a special honor.

Manabu Kohara, Ph.D. in economics from Tokyo University, solver of all the Zen koans (mind puzzles), adviser to captains of industry, writer of books, speaker of seven foreign languages, a paradigm of the great teacher. Wise, good, respected, accomplished. If he didn't have "it" all figured out, then nobody did.

After I was ushered into his private study, we knelt on cushions and bowed our mutual respect. He out of courtesy and I out of awe. For a long time he looked at me and into me.

Very deliberately he shifted his weight to one knee, and just as deliberately reached for his backside and scratched himself in that way and in that place your mother told you was a no-no in public.

"I have hemorrhoids. They hurt and itch."

There was nothing in my mental manual as to how to reply to such an opening remark. I kept my mouth shut and pretended to be thoughtful.

"The hemorrhoids come from stress, you know. From worrying about tourists burning down this firetrap of a temple. From worrying about trying to get enough funding from businessmen to keep it in repair. From arguing with my wife and children, who are not as holy"—he smiled—"as I am. And from despairing over the quality of the lazy young fools who want to be priests nowadays. Sometimes I think I would like to get a little place in Hawaii and just play golf for the rest of my life."

He leaned to one side and scratched himself again.

"It was this way before I was 'enlightened,' you know. And now it is the same after enlightenment."

A long pause while he silently gave me time to consider his words and actions.

Rising, he motioned me to follow him to the entrance alcove of the temple, and we stood before an ancient scroll I had often passed. He said it was time for me to go home, where he felt I had been a "thirsty man looking for a drink and all the while standing knee-deep in a flowing stream." Yes.

Then he read the words of the scroll slowly, first in Japanese and then carefully translated into English:

> *There is really nothing you must be.*
> *And there is nothing you must do.*
> *There is really nothing you must have.*
> *And there is nothing you must know.*
> *There is really nothing you must become.*
> *However. It helps to understand that fire burns,*
>   *and when it rains, the earth gets wet . . .*

"Whatever, there are consequences. Nobody is exempt," said the master.

With a wink, he turned and walked away.

Carefully scratching his backside.

*I*N THE BEGINNING OF BOOKS and at the end of movies, there appear the "credits." Lists of those to whom recognition and appreciation are due. Without whom the book or movie was not possible. In that spirit, as one summer ends, I write my own credits. These people (and some bugs and dogs) made life sing for me with unknowing gifts.

Thanks to the large man in the red dump truck—for the mercy of not blowing his air horn at me while I sat daydreaming through a green light.

Thanks to the small puppy dog trying desperately to make love to a much larger senior lady dog, reminding me that high hopes are part of passion and that lust is often blind. (*The patient toleration of the object of his affection is likewise applauded. What harm?*)

Thanks to the fat, waffled, wrinkled, graying old lady in the faded blue bathing suit, sitting in the children's wading pool in the park on the hottest day of the summer, taking on all comers in a splashing contest—for reminding me of what real beauty is and that childhood can be forever.

Thanks to the small boy in the grocery store who grabbed me from behind around my knees and hugged me and called me "Daddy," and who hugged me once more even when he saw I wasn't his daddy—for handing out free samples of small joy.

Thanks to whoever planted marigolds in the parking strip on Fifteenth Avenue. Not content with making a small piece of no-man's-land beautiful, you added the sign that said: FLOWERS—HAVE SOME.

Thanks to the three young white women playing heads-up, in-your-face, knees-and-elbows-and-take-no-prisoners hard-hat basketball with the young black court hotshots one morning by the lake. And thanks to the young black court hotshots who picked the girls for their team in the first place because they could really play basketball—for showing me that the Equal Rights Amendment is not dead in all the courts of the land.

Thanks to ex-president Jimmy Carter for spending his summer rebuilding houses for poor people with the Humana group. The value of your presidency is still to be judged by history, but the powerful example of your character shines now.

Thanks to the four deaf people speaking sign

language at the market that Saturday, who I knew were telling jokes (*don't know how, but I knew*)—for including me in the laughter without words.

Thanks to the Dixieland band that showed up to play in the park that Sunday afternoon just for the fun of it, and played as if it were a birthday party for everyone on earth—for making me forget that people die.

Thanks to the old geezer playing the harmonica in front of the drugstore downtown, who when asked where to put money, said he didn't do it for the money but for the company, and wore a T-shirt that said: OVER THE HILL AND ON A ROLL—for making me look forward to getting older.

Thanks to the flat-chested young woman at the swimming hole who bravely stood her ground while the policeman wrote her a ticket for indecent exposure for going without her top—and thanks to the policeman who didn't insult her by leaving her out of the arrest procedure when handing out tickets to the more amply endowed—for keeping dignity alive and part of justice.

Thanks to the mailman in my old neighborhood who still remembers my name long after I moved away—for delivering friendliness first and the mail second.

Thanks to the disabled man riding in the electric

wheelchair with the sign on the back: HONK IF YOU'RE HORNY—for reminding me of the courage of good humor.

Thanks to the spiders of August who kept me walking slowly and alert and aware through my garden—morning and evening—for making me see their work and think about my own.

Thanks to the old mongrel dog that came and sat quietly beside me one morning by the lake—for selecting me to receive his silent, undemanding company. I was honored that he would sit by me.

Thanks to the janitor who sings in the halls of the building where I work—for putting "Keep on the Sunny Side" in my mind at day's end.

Thanks to the service-station attendant who washed my car windows anyway, even though I was at the self-service pump—for reminding me that I should not go around not seeing all there is to see.

And there is more. The gifts of the summer were abundant, and there is more news of the world than is reported in the daily paper. And the news is good. The gifts are free.

*T*HERE IS A BENCH IN THE CITY WHERE I LIVE. Its structure is simple—three slabs of smooth gray granite, each six inches thick. The seat piece is sixteen inches wide by forty-two inches long. The two supporting legs are sixteen inches high. Having checked with a compass to be certain, I can tell you that the bench has been carefully aligned so that its long sides face east and west and its two ends point north and south.

This sturdy seat was placed with purpose on the highest ground on the highest hill in my city. So that when the sky is clear on a summer's morning, you can see almost sixty miles in three directions while sitting on the bench.

> *West lies Puget Sound—*
> *East the mighty Cascades run free—*
> *North is the University—*

South, a great tree.
All these things were loved by me.

These words are chiseled into the edge of the bench and are an epitaph. For the bench is, in fact, a tombstone in a cemetery. And I would take you there to sit if I could.

You wouldn't feel uncomfortable sitting on it, I promise. You wouldn't even notice what it was at first. It's right on the edge of a paved lane that curves through the burial grounds, placed so that you are clearly invited to use it. The closest living thing is a dawn redwood tree, comforting in its great age and size—a stout and worthy companion.

The placement of this bench, the words on the edge, the consciousness of the view—all say that someone went to a lot of trouble to be useful in death. A parting gesture of quiet generosity has been made.

In over twenty-five years as a clergyman, I have been involved in hundreds of funerals—in the dying that went before and the burial that came after. There is an inevitable narcissism therein—a focus on self: what I want for MY funeral and what I want done with MY body and what I want for MY epitaph—a very human holding-on to identity as long as breath and granite last. The monuments left behind in the hallowed ground serve to separate the dead from the living and the dead from one another. For me, tombstones are markers of loneliness.

But this bench I speak of is another story. Unique. No name. No conventional epitaph. And no dates. Just an unspoken open invitation for anyone to sit and think. What marks this grave is the gift of silent companionship that bridges loneliness. In all the cemeteries I have visited around the world, I have seen nothing like it—and nothing so fine.

That bench has become a spiritual retreat for me over the years. And I know that I am not the only one to use it, for once I found a note taped under the bench. Not for me; for a young woman from a young man who was in love with her and wrote her careless poetry with great passion. *(No, I'm not sorry I snooped; and yes, I put it back as I found it; and no, I didn't hide in the bushes to see who came for the note. Secret lovers have enough to worry about as it is.)*

Twice I have shared the bench with strangers. I can't explain how we each knew the bench was important to the other and that company was welcome. We just knew, that's all. We sat in silence and went our ways.

And it was on that bench, the summer morning after my fiftieth birthday, that I came to that moment in life when one crosses over from the abstract intellectual knowledge that all human beings die to the active realization that I will die. Me. Fulghum. Will not be. Sooner or later.

Not only did I realize that I will die, but I walked away thinking, Well, it's okay.

I connect that moment of enlightenment with the peculiar sanctuary of the bench and whoever provided it. I accept the challenge of my unknown benefactor to also leave behind some gift for the living instead of a useless stone marking personal real estate.

That bench will last hundreds of years. Many people will sit on it and think not of the name of its owner but of the nameless joys of this sweet life and the mystery of death and how utterly amazing it all is, and that somehow, sometimes, things are just as they should be.

I WRITE TO YOU ON A THURSDAY NIGHT in February, the fortieth day in the year 1989. Winter in Seattle, Washington, USA; clear skies and a new moon.

Though life and stories and writing continue, for now I have come to the place where my work on this volume is done. Tomorrow, the manuscript goes to New York and into the production process that turns it into a book. The letting go is not easy—it's like sending a child off to finishing school.

Some readers may notice that a few of the stories promised on the last page of the *Kindergarten* book did not show up in this one. How come? Answer: Do you ever go off with a long grocery list and come home from the store with a bunch of different stuff? And somebody in the family unsacks the groceries and wants to know why you got this and didn't get that and just where is the whatever? And you want to say, "Well, just be glad I came back, okay?" And the unpacker says, "Well, next time bring what's on the list." Yes, next time I will tell you about frogs, a sign in a grocery store in Pocatello, Idaho, the Salvation Navy, and the smallest circus in the world. Promise.

Pretty soon now I am going to get into my going-to-bed ritual mode. Not unlike yours, I suppose. Walking through the house, I will turn off lights, check latches on doors, turn down the heat, check the refrigerator one more time to see if anything like chocolate ice cream has miraculously appeared there since the last time I looked, around nine o'clock. Then I'll find my way in the dark, by automatic pilot, up the stairs and into bed next to my sleeping wife. There's always a silent laugh at this moment. She wears a black eyeshade, so it's like getting into the sack next to the Lone Ranger. But I always liked the Lone Ranger, and I always say to myself, "The faithful Indian, Tonto, is here." It's my own dumb joke, and I never say it out loud anymore. But I think it. And go to bed amused, which is not such a bad way to turn in for the night, silly joke or no.

Anyway. Next I will get my pillows all shoved around the way I like them, set the alarm, and lie back into that state of being between waking and sleeping. My daytime mind wants to continue sorting the incoming mail and working on the things-to-do list. But I will think to myself, as I have thought as long as I can remember: This day was full—tomorrow's work is for tomorrow. In the meantime, what I need is sleep. Everyone else is asleep, why not me? If I sleep well, the tasks of another day will go well. Sleep, Fulghum, sleep. And I do. This is not exactly a bedtime prayer in the traditional sense, but it supposes peace through the night and a hope for a productive life the next day. Prayer enough, I suppose.

This particular night I go to bed with laughter on my mind. I have read through the manuscript one last time and surprised myself by finding passages that are still funny to me, even after many readings. Humor is a bit suspect—conventional wisdom says it takes away from serious writing. So I wonder if the funny parts should be trimmed out. I think not—and here's why:

To get through this life and see it realistically poses a problem. There is a dark, evil, hopeless side to life that includes suffering, death, and ultimate oblivion as our earth falls into a dying sun. Nothing really matters.

On the other hand, the best side of our humanity finds us determined to make life as meaningful as possible NOW; to defy our fate. Everything matters. Everything.

It is easy to become immobilized between these two points of view—to see them both so clearly that one cannot decide what to do or be.

Laughter is what gives me forward motion at such intersections.

We are the only creatures that both laugh and weep. I think it's because we are the only creatures that see the difference between the way things are and the way they might be. Tears bring relief. Laughter brings release.

Some years ago I came across a phrase in Greek—*asbestos gelos*—unquenchable laughter. I traced it to Homer's *Iliad*, where it was used to describe the laughter of the gods. That's my kind of laughter. And he who laughs, lasts.

Good night. Sleep loose.